# The First Mrs. Solberg

## Volume One

# The First Mrs. Solberg

## Volume One

Michele Menard

The First Mrs. Solberg, Volume 1

By: Michele Menard

Designed by: Darlene Swanson • www.van-garde.com

ISBN: 978-0-9891734-3-8

Published by The Four Menards Publishing, Asheville, NC 28816

TheFourMenards@gmail.com

Printed by Lightning Source, Inc., La Vergne, TN 37086

The Four Menards

A Wrinkle in Rhyme

To my children, who are my life, and to my
grandchildren whom I cannot wait to have.

To my dear Aunt Sis and Uncle Bub!

To Marcia and Cindi - my sisters and my friends!

To Eleanore - I love you in spite of
our different points of view.

To my sensational Aunt Doris and Aunt Maddy.

To Kha, my "cut-up sister from the South!"

To Kazu, my cousin and my friend.

To all who are going through the
agony of a divorce or separation.
My prayers and thoughts are with you.

And last but absolutely not least - To "Elizabeth McBride!"

# Contents

# Chapter One
# Not So Bad, After All!

Sheets of heavy rain lashed against the glass, as majestic palm trees bowed in submission. Across the causeway navy blue waves were rising to the occasion in a regal salute before rushing the shore in crash landings of foam. Battling rebellious umbrellas, people scurried from one point of cover to another in an effort to avoid being drenched.

"Last patient is at 4:00, Regina," mumbled Diane, "and it <u>would</u> have to be a complete dilated exam for contacts!"

"Fine, we can still get to the mall in plenty of time to catch the Easter sales!" Regina felt lighthearted, as though she had finally recovered from her "love 'em and leave 'em" sea captain, Victor Brentzen. Since she had already traveled all over the world as a devoted lay-missionary, Regina decided to take a break with an interim land job. West Palm Beach held just the opportunity as an ophthalmic assistant, in a beautiful four story office building right across the street from the beach. At the age of twenty four, she decided that she would simply avoid men for a good long time, and offered Diane, the office receptionist, her sympathy every time she would announce a new interest in the gender.

Diane Morrison was a tall attractive lady with long curly black hair that was smartly styled in a gypsy cut. She was divorced and had a nine year old son. Always in the market for a new mate, she loved to party. Her dark eyes were thickly lashed to enhance an attractive smile, and she had a very outgoing personality.

Regina Foglietta was a small girl with dark brown eyes and a warm smile. Her thick auburn mass of curls tumbled to the middle of her back when it was not conservatively styled for work. Although she believed that fun was the main ingredient of life, she was not a party person. Enjoying a very close relationship with God and her family, she was down to earth and loved life. Having secured her master level in international ballroom dancing, she was contracted on prestigious cruise-lines as an entertainer and instructor. Free travel opportunity and the large salary that accompanied it, enabled her work with underprivileged people from all over the world.

"It's 4:30 and the patient is still not here," Diane whined.

"Well, he can reschedule if he's much later," Regina turned in response to the bell on the door.

Frank Solberg entered announcing himself as a science teacher who was to start medical school in August, and needed glasses and contact lenses. With one smart snap, his umbrella collapsed to a quarter of its' original size. Pleased with himself, he indicated the compact object and said, "My light saber."

The two ladies exchanged an unimpressed, disgusted look

and signed the patient in. It was one thing to be delayed for shopping as a result of an eye emergency and quite another for a pompous man, who was irresponsibility late, and clearly equipped with a Jedi complex.

Regina had a talent for being sarcastic and could have won a first prize in the history taking and screening portion of the exam. Frank Solberg, however, found her completely amusing, and enjoyed every minute of the professional demeanor flavored with ever so subtle verbal abuse.

Sending the glaring sun to wave a surrender flag, the Florida storm retreated as dramatically as it had appeared. "The weather's tantrum is over; look at that sun," one of the patients who was signing out was relieved. Regina offered to stay over so Diane could run ahead to the mall, and planned to meet her there after the patient left. Finally leaving, Frank Solberg blinked wildly at the sun pouring through the huge front windows that lined the reception area. "Exactly how am I supposed to drive home with my eyes dilated?" he asked. "Well, one who is preparing for medical school might know better than to come for such an exam as the only driver and more than a half an hour late to boot," sighed Regina, obviously anxious to finish closing the office.

"May I wait for awhile until the sun at least goes down a little?"

"Umm, sure I guess that would be okay," she forced a hint of pleasantry into her answer. Remembering her initial risk management training, she saw no alternative. What harm could it be anyway if he sat and monitored the sun level while she finished cleaning instruments and straightening magazines?

Frank Solberg was a tall, well built man, with conservatively cut sandy blonde hair and dark brown eyes. Taking a seat that provided a full view of the ophthalmic technician who had dowsed his eyes to begin with, he positioned himself comfortably, watching her work.

After a brief time and an amicable chat, the sun dropped sufficiently for safe driving. Fishing his keys out of his pocket, Frank inquired as to the possibility of continuing the conversation another time. Still thinking about the Easter sales, Regina scribbled her number on an appointment card, bid the "not- so- bad- after-all-patient" farewell, and booked it to the mall.

By the time Regina burst through the door of her temporary home with her mother, stepfather, and youngest sister, the three were finishing up their dinner. "Well, look who's here," chuckled her stepfather, "how about a plate of dinner, honey?" Dan McBride was a tall, bulky, architect with a good hearted nature, an easy laugh, and eight collective adult children. Four were his own biological creations and four belonged to his second wife, Elizabeth. Formerly a widower, he sincerely loved both his prior family and new extensions to the same. Regina was third from the youngest. "No thanks, Dad," she answered, "Diane and I ate at the Orange Blossom. Look what I got for three bucks," she added nodding to her youngest sister, Andrea. "Wow," Andrea complemented the purse, "neat color."

"I'm glad you like it, be-caaauuse this one is yours, and it can't be returned." The jubilation was interrupted by the telephone, and their mother summoning Regina.

"Frank who? Oh, oh yes, how are you? I'm glad you got home all right. Well, I'm not certain, let me check." During the brief hesitation, Regina noted that she was being closely observed by the other three people in the room. "Well I guess that would be okay. Fine then, I'll see you at 6:30 Saturday night." Hanging up the phone, Regina was already asking herself out loud why she committed to go out with Frank Solberg, whom she had already been annoyed with once today.

Dan's eyes lit up, "So did I hear correctly? Our little Pandemonium is finally going to let go of Poseidon and try giving some other prospective man a chance?" *Pandemonium* was his loving nickname for this dedicated missionary, who had proved to be the wild uproar that the name implied! Always overflowing with energy, as soon as she entered a setting, it sprang to action.

"I am not sure yet, Dad," Regina laughed, "this guy has the makings of a problem: future doctor, present Jedi, late for his appointment, and a current science teacher somewhere in North Palm Beach."

"And the down side?" asked Andrea.

"I'm still in love with Victor and the sea," Regina answered quietly.

"Well, I'm off to Uncle Bub's. I want to show Aunt Sis my bag of bargains."

Aunt Sis and Uncle Bub, correctly named Larry and Madeline Camerson, lived three doors down in the same Wellington town house complex. They were very close to Bub's sister and their new brother-in-law, not to mention all eight of their kids. Regina quickly handed Elizabeth and Dan each a bargain Cross pen set and was out the door.

Dan yawned and remarked to his wife, "Elizabeth, it has been a long haul for her. I can only hope that she gives this fellow a try. It's time for Regina to stop globetrotting and settle down. Look at the gifts she has brought each of us on an unmarked Tuesday. You'd think she was Santa. I would love to see her find someone who will take care of her for a change. Andrea, I hope you'll help us cheerlead this!"

"Dad, she just met him today, and doesn't appear to even like him. Regina hates concerts and from what I could hear, that's to be their first date. I don't hear  wedding bells pealing madly, at the moment. She's also scheduled to leave again in the fall for the Netherlands. She loves to dance and loves her missionary work even more.  Regina has a long overdue, wonderful life, and she will eventually get over Captain Heartache," Andrea popped the last of her desert into her mouth. "Well a man can still hope," Dan looked over at his wife.

Regina was brushing her hair when the doorbell rang. She could hear her parents introducing themselves and Andrea, but was in no rush to leave her room. Asking herself why she was dating anyone, she pulled the front of her hair up and secured it with a turquoise barrette that matched her dress. Hugging the giant teddy bear that occupied her rocking chair, she closed her eyes and listened to the birds outside of her bedroom window. Wondering if it was too late to "call in sick," she fastened her earrings and walked into the living room. Frank was stunned to see her, as she looked even more beautiful out of the printed scrubs she wore to work. He was dressed in a smart navy suit with a starched shirt and tie. Standing, he handed his date a bouquet of spring flowers. Touched by the gesture, Regina was slightly stunned, as she had not realized how handsome he was.

The concert was by Maynard Ferguson, Canadian Jazz musician and trombone player. Frank explained that both he and his brother had played the trombone in college, and were still alumni marching band members. Following the performance, the couple walked along the beach and talked.

Brilliant stars filled the black velvet sky, upstaged only by a bright full moon. Easy waves provided a continuation of the evening's music as they lined the shore with sparkling foam.

Regina was pleasantly surprised to learn that Frank Solberg was a lot of fun to be with – as a friend. Hoping to make it perfectly clear that she was interested in nothing more, she stressed her future plans to sail to the Netherlands in the fall, where she would assist underprivileged families who were building farms. Recognizing a sore subject, Frank proceeded with caution.

Frank had learned that morning, that Dan and Bub played on the same golf course as his family did. Seeking more information from the mutual friend, he learned that Regina was not the type to be pushed and had recently been devastated by a sea captain. Charmed even further to learn that her stepfather's nickname for her was *Pandemonium,* he decided to bide his time, hope for the best, and pray every chance that he could that this Netherland project would never materialize. During their meeting this evening, Dan had invited Frank and his father to join him and Bub at the country club for golf next Saturday, and he would surely learn more then.

Frank escorted Regina to her door, and lingering, thanked her for the "honor" of dating her. Inviting him in for coffee, she returned the compliment, as they talked easily about their futures. He had graduated from the University of Florida and was an addicted Gator fan! Awaiting entrance to medical school at the University of Miami, he was teaching Science and Chemistry classes for a private academy in North Palm Beach. The couple talked until 2:00 am, and although, neither of them seemed to be tired, they realized that they must end their date. Regina walked Frank to the door, where he kissed her lightly. Bowing graciously, he thanked her again. Alright, he was a nice person, but that was not going to interfere with her travel plans!

Next thing Regina knew, Mrs. Solberg was calling Elizabeth to extend an invitation for a cook out at their home after the golf game next Saturday. March in Florida was typically warm, so Regina and her sister opted to wear sundresses for the occasion.

The Solbergs' house which was formerly a large triplex with a huge fenced in yard, was set back at the end of a long, well kept driveway, bordered with spring flowers. Meticulously trimmed Avocado trees, each supporting a German bird house, lined the back fence. Along the side fences, orange and grapefruit trees rivaled each other with delightful citrus aromas, as a gentle fountain introduced the full length stone patio that boasted an exotic orchid display.

Inside the house, walled in deep beige and terra cotta granite, were comfortable couches and easy chairs set on area rugs complimenting well polished wood floors. Large paddle fans hummed pleasantly from the sky lighted ceiling, as the living room opened widely to introduce the dining area. Sporting an antique oak table and chairs that seated sixteen guests effortlessly, the room was warm and welcoming. Light reflected off a faceted crystal fruit bowl in the center of the table, while a matching collection of fine crystal glasses winked at the guests from an oak framed glass cabinet.

Mrs. Solberg was a gourmet cook and her kitchen reflected her talents. Large circular racks housing polished copper bottom pots and pans of every size, hung over an island of chopping blocks. The state of the art stove and refrigerator were set against the earth toned walls separated by a large window dressed in cheerful Mediterranean style curtains.

The four bedrooms were excluded from the tour, as they were occupied by the extensive selection of pets who resided with the Solbergs, usually having full run of the territory.

The families seemed to enjoy each other and the steak and Caesar salad dinner followed by Mrs. Solberg's homemade cream puffs, was splendid. The two mothers exchanged recipes and the fathers talked golf, while the younger people were busy admiring the ancient orchid collection.

In the weeks that followed, Frank and Regina would meet after work, <u>as friends</u>, and go to the beach, have a picnic, see a movie, or eat dinner with at each other's temporary homes. While apple-boarding along the beach one week before the mark of their third month of dating, they decided to take a break. Tossing the Frisbee that Frank had painted for her in the sun, moon, and stars pattern, was the obvious choice for the post sunset activity. Regina jumped up to catch the disc, and noticed a note taped to the bottom of it. She removed the paper and read: "Would you settle for a trip to the Netherlands after I am a rich doctor? I will help with the farms. Please say yes!"

P.S. "My parents have permanently banned their army of cats from the dining room table!"

It wasn't long at all before Frank Solberg and his parents, Dorothy and Raymond, had fallen in love with Regina. Suffice to say that both families were secretly hoping that Frank would get a yes to the big question next Tuesday on the three month anniversary of when they met. Frank's only brother, Adam, did not like the idea. He felt that an engagement followed by a mere three months of dating was ludicrous, especially to such a wild card. He was also concerned that this Regina had a very close relationship with God and minced no words with mortals on His behalf.

Dorothy Solberg was an assertive, outgoing lady with a pleasant but controlling personality. The height of a small dinosaur, she was still attractive.

Raymond Solberg, a stock broker, was considerably shorter than his wife and graciously accepted the fact that she wore the pants in their small family of four.

Adam Solberg, a veterinarian by force, cleverly disguised any inconvenience to his field as dedication. His parents had adopted numerous stray animals and were exceptionally kind to them. To Adam's obvious resentment, each new comer wound up in his clinic as a walk in, for a free examination, spay or neuter, worm and flea treatment, and a complete set of shots. After all, he was educated on mommy and daddy's nickel and held his practice rent free in one of their many office buildings!

Regina could not help enjoying his annoyance with the situation that he had gotten himself into. While she was very polite to Adam, she was not fond of him. His wife, Marge, was a pacifist in every sense of the word, who ruffled no feathers and rolled with the tide at any cost. While she was amused by Regina's open description of the Solberg house, as *Noah's Ark in dry dock,* she was careful not to join in the laughter.

Marge was delighted to see that not everyone was intimidated by the Solbergs or their money. She coveted Regina's comical ability to mention the huge cat, who made her bed in the crystal fruit bowl, and the shameless parading of the remaining eleven felines across the table during dinner. Highlighted by large clumps of hair blown across the living room floor by the paddle fans; these cats created a setting that could easily nauseate the homeless. Full time housekeepers applied and resigned, as if through a revolving door.

Regina looked up from the creek in front of her parent's townhouse, lingering to enjoy the sound of the water rushing over the sun bleached rocks. Thoughts swirled through her head like a graceful white tornado, as she had managed to fall in love with Frank Solberg!  She found, to her great surprise, that real love, was hardly like the fairy tale she had always mistaken it to be. Having underestimated the feeling of a complete bond with another person, she prayed out loud, "Father, he's a sweetheart, but not at all the prince in shining armor that I have been waiting for. Moreover, I'm not really much of a princess, but we both seem to have that secret ingredient that neither one of us can live without.  We both love You, and want to serve You. Is it unusual that this happened so quickly, Lord? Are we on the right track?"

Dan came out on the second story deck to shout down the time. "Just another moment," she answered, and continued her conversation, "God, please let this relationship go according to Your will. I love Frank but I'm not sure that I am ready to give up my travel to be a doctor's wife. Please stay by my side and guide me. Bless both of our families and all who would be affected by our future decisions, and please give me the wisdom to deal with his family and to understand and encourage his love for them. Now for my favorite part, ' Lord, please help me to remember that nothing is going to happen to me today, that You and I together can't handle.'"

Steak and Ale was a quiet restaurant with a great menu. Regina, having a passion for artichokes, naturally ordered one. Frank loved teasing her about doing her nails to, "dig in the bushes!"

"Perhaps you should try them, she had advised on multiple occasions; artichokes dipped in olive oil are delicious."

"No thank you, I'll stick to civilized food," Frank could not resist the amusement with his "<u>friend.</u>"

While "digging in the bushes," Regina thought she found a piece of glass staring up at her. Frazzled, she removed it to discover a breathtaking solitary diamond ring. Frank took it and wiped it off with the linen napkin. Dropping down on one knee, he proposed to her, while the other diners stood up and applauded. The emotional moment was broken by laughter, as a little old man knelt up on his chair and shading his eyes asked loudly, "What did she say?"

The following Saturday, both families including Bub and Sis, met for a big celebration dinner, and to Regina's shock, voted to push the scheduled December wedding to August! The Solbergs wanted the newlyweds to be completely settled to avoid distraction during medical school, which they reminded everybody present was extremely expensive. The Mc Brides were afraid that given the hustle bustle of Jackson Memorial Hospital and the hectic life in Miami, Regina might reconsider her engagement and return to her missionary life on the sea.

Regina remained composed while holding back the tears caused by the stress set upon her. The ice rink on her left hand seemed to be changing into a ball and chain, and Frank picked up on this immediately. He raised his glass in a toast to his new fiancée. "Let us give thanks to God for sending Regina into our lives and ask Him to personally oversee the wedding plans as He sees fit. Regina, sweetheart, it will be a December wedding unless you feel the need to push it forward."

# Chapter Two
# My! Miami

The typical quirks found in wedding planning were compounded by the rush of the date advance. There were eighteen attendants to include all siblings. Andrea, the maid of honor, was fiercely protective of the bride- to-be, and had her stepfather's backing. Mrs. Solberg was a piece of work to deal with, and it was no secret that Elizabeth McBride could be very protective of her daughters and would gladly engage in a confrontation on their behalf if necessary. Adam was the best man.

Exhausted by petty arguing, Andrea slumped into a living room chair. Dan looked up from his blueprint, "What's up, sweetheart?"

Near tears, Andrea disclosed the new dilemma. Each of the mothers had purchased a pair of bride and groom champagne glasses for the wedding toast. Fighting over which was to be used, Elizabeth consulted her etiquette book, revealing the appropriate duties of the mother-of-the-bride. Bitter realization caused Dorothy to threaten a telephone call to Regina for the purpose of blurting out the details of the upcoming surprise bridal shower.

Having followed through with her plan, the mother-in-law to be called Andrea to tell her that the shower was not going to be a surprise after all!  Dorothy ended the conversation by standing her ground on the issue of the glasses, as hers were purchased first.

An outraged Elizabeth insisted that she was going to see that her set of glasses had their place at the reception that THEY WERE PAYING FOR! Dan laughed quietly, as Bub came through the door to discuss the tee time for Sunday.

"Well, what's up maid of honor?" Given a brief summary of what had occurred, Bub laughed too. Andrea was relieved to see that the two men were in agreement that the behavior of both mothers was ridiculous. "Two questions," Dan help up his fingers, "Can you keep a secret and do we have a pillow case that your mother wouldn't miss if it disappeared?"

"Yes and yes," Andrea answered.  After Bub was also sworn to secrecy,

Dan got up from his chair and collected both sets of glasses, while Andrea snatched the pillow case. Placing all four glasses carefully in the pillow case, he held it closed at the top, and extended it in mid air. Handing Bub a golf trophy from the den, he said, "Swing on three my brother, one, two, three!"

The blow shattered all four glasses as Andrea, laughing too hard to talk, took the pillow case from Dan. The architect whispered, "Now let's get out of here before your mother comes home! We'll toss these in the dumpster at my office and have a sundae as we plan our explanation for their disappearance." The three culprits left through the back door.

Over ice cream the they decided that the broken glasses could have been knocked over accidentally by one of the housekeepers. Since the responsible party would feel bad enough, there was no point in mentioning it, so Dan simply replaced them with a set very similar to the ones that Elizabeth had rightfully selected. Bub laughed as he asked, "Where do you buy those?"

"Hallmark usually has them," Andrea was still laughing herself, "that's where Mom and I got the last set, anyway."

"So we'll stop on the way home and get a similar set," Dan finished the last of his sundae.

While nobody believed the story, it ended the argument and checked further petty issues. Regina didn't like surprises anyway, so she was far more delighted with the champagne glass saga, than the original bridal shower plan.

Reverend Patrick Dain, an Episcopalian priest and childhood friend of Dan McBride's, was delighted to perform the wedding ceremony.

On August 25, 1979, Regina Louise Foglietta, became Mrs. Frank Solberg without reservations. Their wedding song was Simon and Garfunkle's *Bridge Over Troubled Water*, reflecting their commitment to each other and to the field of medicine. Following the exchange of vows, there wasn't a dry eye in the church.

The reception was not only spectacular, but a great deal of fun for everyone. Guests mingled, danced, and feasted on a grand buffet which included a large assortment of hot and cold dishes, various salads, and an international array of breads, rolls, and pas-

tries. Exquisitely presented, the six tiered wedding cake, supported clusters of frosted grapes cascading down the sides. Cherub
couples, sculpted from sugar, occupied a seat on each cluster,
while the top layer displayed two graceful, white feathered doves
jointly holding a wedding band.

During the festivities, Frank and Regina presented their
parents with touching poems, The Parents of the Bride, and The
Parents of the Groom, which they had written and laminated on
handsome cherry wood plaques. Following that, every member
of the bridal party enjoyed both a sincere gift of appreciation, as
well as a gag gift presentation. Some of the bridal party had arranged a roast that addressed the entire wedding planning process. There was not a guest who wasn't doubled over laughing,
including Father Dain.

After their honeymoon at Sandpiper Bay, the couple moved into
a one bedroom condominium on the eighth floor of the Isla Del
Mar, overlooking the Miami River. While the apartment was located close to the hospital, it was unfortunately surrounded by
undesirable neighborhoods.

Isla Del Mar was a group of five enormous buildings, in the shape
of a star. Each building was ten stories high and had an eat-in-
café on the ground floor, that was combined with a small grocery
store. The structure was built to allow the river to surround it,
enabling the only entrance to be over a gated bridge, staffed 24
hours daily by an armed security guard.

In the center of the buildings was a large Olympic sized

swimming pool and huge patio area. The condo belonged to the Solbergs, and was to be the property of the bride and groom if: <u>fol-lowing medical school, Frank selected an internship and resident program in Miami</u>. Regina decided to bring as much light to as many people as she could during their committed four year stay in this high crime location, which was at best, a potential war zone.

International doll collecting was Regina's hobby, and the contents decorated their new home, along with Frank's Florida Gator paraphernalia. Photos of Regina's competition dancing, the Florida Gator Marching Band, and foreign missionary adven-tures, enhanced the surroundings, depicting a typical combina-tion of two very different lives, now bonded together as one.

Flea market curtains and couch pillows were as admired by the McBrides, as they were loathed by the Solbergs. Dorothy Solberg was annoyed by the neglected display of their fine crystal wedding gifts, and angered by the photographs of Regina danc-ing with other men, professionals or no. She felt that even the missionary work preserved in photos, should be eliminated.

In short, Regina should let go of her former life in exchange for the promising future that lie ahead. Frank's pictures with fe-male band members, displayed in Dorothy's own needle point frames, were unrelated to the issue. After all, they were his college shots and the future was a continuation of this story.

The modest furniture included a second hand dinette set, which to Dorothy, was a glorified card table, and the yard sale centerpiece was not helping her mood. She asked the young cou-ple what they were thinking. "Frank, exactly what do you call this décor, or lack-there-of?"

"It's what we have to work with, Mom. I think the dolls are exquisite and our personal items are cheerful to look at as well. There are six other medical students in this building, on government loans, whose homes are not nearly as nicely decorated as ours."

"So you have no theme, no taste, and no pride. Exactly what statement are you making, Regina, by displaying these dance pictures?"

Regina quickly closed her eyes in prayer. "God, if you could please tip her off the balcony even though the railing is sturdy, ... Please give me the wisdom to handle this situation in Your love."

"Mom, we have taste that matches our budget. Our home is done in *Early Med School*. If it wasn't for you and Dad, we wouldn't have such a nice place to live.

If my dancing photos and travel pictures upset you, than they will be boxed and kept in the closet.  How would that be?"

"That would be better, Regina, but we are offended that the crystal is not displayed. Your hideous dolls are certainly getting enough attention. Don't you think you should grow up? Dolls? Really, Regina!"

Frank could stand no more, "Mother, it is not necessary to speak to her that way, and her doll collection is just as important to her as my things are to me. The apartment will remain as it is."

Observing Dorothy storm out onto the patio balcony, she appealed again,"Now would be good, Lord. She's leaning, .... O.K. I'll behave, but Father, please stay right here by me!"

"Frank, let us take the dance pictures down and consolidate the dolls to display the crystal on the top shelf."

"Then she wins."

"No, Frank, He does. Missionaries live by a code; no un-necessary roughness."

Mr. Solberg, having joined his wife, was now in tears. Regina recognized the opportunity at once and glanced up to the sky, "I love You this much, Abba."

She walked out onto the balcony and asked her in-laws inside.

"Mom and Dad, we do not have your decorating skills yet, so please forgive us. We are going to store all of the dancing pictures, and were wondering if you could help us rearrange the dolls so that we may display the crystal properly on the top shelf where it will be safe. In addition, I am not the fabulous cook that you are, Mom, so maybe you can give me some tips with the kitchen?"

Dorothy was overwhelmed, Raymond delighted, and Frank puzzled. The entire scenario had changed. How was Regina able to just call on God so freely, and what had caused this immediate solution that had his parents eating out of her hand? Love. She had said it a million times during the planning of the wedding.

"When someone is speaking unkindly, the instant we respond in anger, we are at very best, as bad as they are. Make no mistake about it - missionaries are not doormats, but warriors. There is no greater weapon than love."

The travel and dance pictures were packed, and the Solbergs insisted on getting a nicer cabinet for Regina's dolls and the crystal. The furniture store was called and the delivery arranged.

" Regina, darling, would it be intrusive if we offered to take you two *"Early Med School"* decorators to the Rusty Pelican for dinner? Mom assures me that your wine stew will be better tomorrow and can be kept in the crock pot in the refrigerator."

"Sure, that would be wonderful, Dad, thank you."

Frank was beaming with pride and expectation that he too,

would grow to know God on this personal level. After all, He did win, and He always would.

The week before medical school started, Regina landed herself a job at the world renowned Bascom Palmer Eye Institute, affiliated with Jackson Memorial Hospital. Excited that she would be working not only with private patients, but with indigent patients as well, she enthusiastically placed her uniforms on hangers. Thinking about her safety commuting, Frank was happy that they had sold her car for budget purposes and would share his. In addition, he was worried that Regina may be overwhelmed by the surroundings of her new place of employment.

The doting Solberg seniors got wind of their son's concerns during one of their multiple daily phone calls, and popped in again, unexpectedly for dinner. They insisted on taking the newlyweds to Kelly's Seafood and wasted no time attempting to redirect Regina's employment plans to a private practice away from the hospital. Dorothy had already taken the liberty to arrange an interview with a personal friend of the family's who happened to be the office manager.

Regina was very independent, and did not appreciate the interference regardless of the good intentions involved. Frank, caught between a rock and a hard place, was not certain which approach would be best. Dorothy began her campaign sweetly but her voice got increasingly bossy. "Regina, Frank cannot concentrate on his studies if he must worry about you. What possessed you to sell your car without asking Dad and me? You are being selfish and unreasonable, dear. Frank, what do you think? Are we asking too much for you two kids to cooperate with us since we are spending an obscene amount of money on your education? We will be glad to subsidize your budget so that Regina need not work at all, or we will get her another car with the understanding that she will not work on or near the hospital complex."

Frank was obviously not used to arguing with his parents, and Regina loved him too much to see him in this uncomfortable position. She therefore answered for him. "Mom, I appreciate your concern for Frank's classes and for my safety as well. Please consider that I have traveled all over the world as a missionary, and that I have been in some very frightening places. There is no need to subsidize our budget, and I'm serving notice on all of you that I am not made of spun sugar, nor am I careless. I too, have a calling here, and I intend to answer it."

The Solbergs laughed, but they were far from happy with the outcome of their own mission this evening. Frank could no longer conceal the pride in his new wife, and Dorothy saw it written all over his face. How dare this religious little ingrate speak to them that way! Was that a fondness she noticed in Raymond as well? She would deal with that on the way home. Why, Adam and Marge would have jumped at her generous offer. Perhaps a meeting with Regina's parents would solve this problem.

Although Elizabeth McBride was by nature a *people person*, when backed into a corner she could be easily ignited. Well aware of a potential problem, Dan stepped in to keep things in perspective. With a diplomacy that was second to none, it was said that he could 'tell a man to go to hell so that he looked forward to the trip!' He not only agreed to the meeting, but invited the Solbergs out to dinner. He opened the conversation by letting everyone know that Frank and Regina were aware of their dinner plans and the purpose of them. He added that since the two "kids" are adults, he felt that they had a right to know.

Dan had a very entertaining way of speaking, and in addition, had the gift of making everyone feel like they were the only key to the potential problem. He clarified that Regina was one of Elizabeth's four children and that the former family of five were accustomed to living on a very slim budget.

"Michael Foglietta, was a dear man who drove a taxi in the Bronx. He was killed in a crash leaving Elizabeth with four young children – Sophie, Regina, Michael, and Andrea, to raise by herself. The devastated family had struggled and succeeded. Sophie, thanks to scholarships, had become a Pharmacist, Michael was a promising attorney, by the same methods, and Andrea was headed for her degree in Sociology. Three of the kids accomplished their goals as a result of hard work and a drive that would rival the toughest!"

Regina, since the age of thirteen, had worked in nursing homes, to help with the bills. Despite being sentenced to Catholic school for twelve years, she never fit in there, and was labeled as the *different* Foflietta. Like her father, Regina had a very irreverent sense of humor which was not appreciated by the Catholic priests and nuns of the times. She detested school and all of the work that came along with it, and consequently, was granted no scholarships. She was a steadfast strength to her family, however, and had earned their respect as the same. She worked ridiculous hours, walked to the grocery store, and prepared tasty low cost meals and baked goods. She kept little if any of her earnings for herself, and all through high school and well after, had no real life of her own.

Noting that the entire party was intrigued, Dan continued his story, explaining that he and Elizabeth met after their children were adults and only Andrea lived at home. Once Elizabeth no longer needed her, Regina set out to do God's work on the high seas, enabling her to travel expense free. Turning down valuable complimentary tours, she would seek out the poor people of other nations, and used her income to help them. Regina was ruffled by nothing, and viewed life as a dashing bold adventure. She was a self taught dancer who had previously finalized her international training at an Arthur Murray Dance studio in Columbus, Ohio. She paid for her advanced lessons with former champions, with earnings from a nursing home job on the night shift. Making ends meet, she also worked as an A&W cook on Saturdays and Sundays.

Regarded by her family as a mere flitter in the dancing business, they were shocked when Bub and Sis dropped over for coffee, carrying the *Miami Herald*. Highlighted in the advertizing section they read: current US ballroom champions, Regina Foglietta and Jeffery Winters, will be flown in from Columbus, Ohio, to accept an invitation as the opening act for the Barbara McNair show at the Ocean Front Theater in Miami.

Dan, who was new in the picture and had not met Regina, arranged for the whole family to see the show in Miami. They were astounded to see her name in lights and the excellent performance that rated the privilege. After the show it was announced that the rising young dance team had been booked on continuing world cruises as entertainers and ballroom instructors.

Elizabeth McBride bitterly added her disappointment that Regina had no degree, and would now be running all over the world spending money on underprivileged people.

Dan flashed a broad smile at his mesmerized audience, "Regina has a PHD from the "school of hard knocks." We need to remember that she adores God and loves her husband with all of her heart. I applaud your efforts to protect her, Dorothy and Raymond, and we love you for them. However, if we attempt to block Regina from her missionary work, not only will we be unsuccessful, but we will surely find that she can be very difficult to deal with."

While the Solbergs saw Regina in a new light and agreed that further meddling would not be wise, Dorothy was uneasy about losing control of the "kids."

"Dan, what if we make one more request containing a fabulous offer? If Regina still resists, we'll just leave it alone."

"That sounds fine to me, Dorothy, what about you, Elizabeth; does that sound good to you?" Elizabeth shrugged her shoulders indifferently.

"Very good then, Raymond, we will draft a letter and see what we can do."

The dinner continued pleasantly, the focus switched to golf and cooking.

Dorothy mailed the letter that night.

Dear Frank,

As you were told, we had dinner with the McBrides tonight. We all salute your adulthood, but <u>we</u> are still paying for your education, Frank, and expect you to govern yourself accordingly. Bascom Palmer Eye Institute is not an option for Regina.

Your father and I are not about to entertain any added stress. Please review the following offer and mail your response in writing:

We must insist that Regina work away from the JMH complex or accept compensation and not work at all. We will buy her another car, as we have already offered to do. In addition we will provide you kids with an American Express card so that you can go out to eat weekly at our expense. We consider this a fair and reasonable offer.

Love,
Mom and Dad

RESPOND BELOW:

While Frank and Regina were still laughing about the letter, Chuck and Jeannie Nugent came down for nachos. Chuck was from Texas and started medical school with Frank. His wife Jeannie, was just hired as nurse in the psychiatric ward at JMH. Living upstairs would make studying together both fun and convenient.

"Hey, Chuck, read this nonsense."

"I'm glad that I'm going through on student loans. I would rather owe greenbacks than my flippin soul."

"There is a limit to how much I will allow my parents to dis-respect Regina."

"I would tell your folks to pound salt, brother. They are way out of line."

"No can do –'un-necessary roughness.'"

"What is your answer going to be then?"

"I don't know yet, but Regina thinks we should just leave it for awhile. By then she will be settled in at BPEI and the matter will probably resolve itself."

"You know what they say, 'the difference between in-laws and outlaws is that outlaws are wanted.'"

Jackson Memorial was a city in itself and BPEI was nose to nose with the rest of the complex. The monumental structures, reaching for the sky, stretched out in all directions. Ambulances and the monorail provided the music that white coats fluttered around by, like leaves on a windy fall day. Lives were continuously at risk and the adrenaline pumped through the air. Oddly the hustle was not accompanied by chaos. Everyone who was supposed to know what they were doing seemed to, omitting confusion from the scenario. Free entertainment was occasionally provided when the majestic Concord soared straight up against the sapphire sky, leaving spectators breathless.

Frank and Regina stayed very busy and very happy. Money for all of the medical students was tight, but nobody seemed to want for anything. They had pot luck dinner groups rotating houses on a versatile schedule. The menus were budget friendly and the evenings always promised a lot of laughs and support.

Regina was no stranger to penny pinching and thoroughly enjoyed her crock pot specials. Her abilities to blend in at BPEI and with the other medical students' wives, kept their social life more active than they needed it to be! The young Solbergs were fun to be around and did not engage in gossip under any circumstances. Consequently, they were exempt from the usual hospital drama, and respected for their ability to be in that position.

While Frank spent countless hours studying, Regina threw herself whole-heartedly into her missionary life. Her first passion was the indigent clinic. The patients were very poor and often referred to as "dirt balls." Many were prisoners who had engaged in a fight that resulted in eye trauma. The halls were packed with these patients who were sentenced to wait for hours to see a doctor. Children were screaming and crying while short fused adults responded to them harshly. They were often hungry and thirsty with no means of satisfaction, as the cafeteria was far too expensive and the overcrowded water fountains were far away from their waiting area. Magazines and books were reserved for the paying patients, and sadness and depression hung in the air, as the burdened herd graciously accepted the fact that they were entitled to absolutely no dignity.

Appealing to the local grocery known as X-tras, Regina scheduled an appointment with the manager. Bargaining for packages of two huge turkey legs, she secured a bulk deal at twenty cents each. She had institutional sized boxes of cookies donated, not to mention gigantic bags of lollipops. Purchasing 5 pound cans of peanut butter and jelly were also cost effective. Next stop was the day old bread store where one could buy a loaf of bread for ten cents. The flea market served as another hot spot for large Tupperware containers, additional crock pots, and a collapsible grocery cart. Large boxes of toys were purchased and disinfected.

The crock pots worked overtime, piloted by Regina and Jeannie, cooking the turkey legs for the freezer. Each morning before clinic, Regina would rise at 4:00 am, to make peanut butter and jelly and turkey salad sandwiches for the patients. Loading up her cart, she made multiple trips, transporting the supplies to the ground floor of the BPEI. The hospital administrator signed a requisition for five gallon coolers of water which became lemonade with a swift ladling of economical powdered mix. Within a few weeks the patients were organized, and much happier. Burned out staff also became considerably easier to deal with. Children's activity centers were set up to reduce the noise and to keep the halls and aisles clear.

Only one staff member opposed Regina. Nurse Frances McNeal, a tall thin cross looking lady, wore her silver hair glued in a bagel shape at the base of her neck. Formerly an army nurse, she was in charge of the clinic, and believed that it should have stiff surroundings. McNeal was determined to stop, "Pollyanna," dead in her tracks.

Regina got wind of her nickname, which only amused her. Recalling the shy intern who had crossed her opposition a few months ago, she decided that she was in good company. The unfortunate young man had mistakenly addressed the head nurse as Nurse O'Neal, and had his head snapped off for the error.

"O'Neal down and kiss my butt," the cranky RN yelled. "You'll be put on report for this!" McNeal had since become known as "Nurse Ratched," by the rotating medical students.

Regina's hard work continued un-noticed for many months. Eventually medical students realized that they could partake in a free turkey sandwich, with all of the ghetto trimmings. Occasionally an attending physician would even dine with the group. The area became known as "Lunch at Pollyanna's." Doctors stopping by for lunch would often acknowledge the patients, setting them at ease. Frank Solberg, armed with life like puppets from his wife's doll collection, became known as Mr. Science, as a result of his lunch presentations to the clinic children. Eventually it was common knowledge that doctors who had lollipop sticks extending from their mouths were also nicer to deal with.

Earning a medal for bravery, Regina approached Nurse McNeal with a turkey salad sandwich, cookies, and a cup of lemonade. "Nurse McNeal, I wondered if I may ask you to sample our lunch and give us your honest criticism, since you are known as perfection." Regina, who was never discouraged by being ignored, continued. "All of the children here admire you. Chelsea Garcia, from the weekly roster, made herself a little paper cap, to play nurse in the clinic while she waits her turn." Nurse McNeal glared at Regina and motioned her away. "This clinic was a fine operation before you came dancing in with your sunshine and nonsense, Solberg. Everyone is laughing at you behind your back, you idiot!"

"But laughing!  Here inside these walls people are laughing. This clinic was a "fine operation," because of your expertise and good order. No sunshine newcomer, toting a sandwich cart and a modest box of toys accomplished that!

The quality had to be here first to make this whole thing fly. Like it or not you are the key to the laughter here and nothing less than impressive."

"Solberg, keep God to yourself. I do not want to belong to your asinine operation. Why don't you get busy before I put you on report?"

"Listen, Ms. McNeal, I am busy. Busy being amused that someone as intelligent as you are; would think that anyone can keep God to themselves. You're His, just as I am. If you don't like it, then you take that up with Him. Make no mistake about it, ma'am, you already do belong to this operation. You are in fact the vital foundation of it. Children here want to emulate you; now the choice to ignore it; well that's all your own."

Later in the day, Regina spotted the paper plate that held "Nurse Ratched's" lunch, in the trash can. Empty.

"Solberg, if you wish to turn this place into a fast food facility, get that hair up off your collar. Don't just stand there, here are some pins! Following that, wash your hands thoroughly and report to the cafeteria. They will be donating all of our paper goods from now on! Understood?"

"Ma'am, yes ma'am!" Regina was close to tears. "You did it Abba," she whispered. Thanks for letting me a part of Your work. Did I mention today, how much I love you?"

"Nurse Ratched," now enjoyed her name and went by it. "Pollyanna," did not especially care for hers, but what the heck!

The following week, Frank was off early due to a cancelled lecture, and wandered over to pick his wife up from work. Visibly startled he asked, "Polly, is that Nurse Ratched that I see wearing her hair in a French twist and smiling? Nurse Ratched, who could teach Frigid One and Two? Nurse Ratched, who could stop a freight train with her mere expression? What have you done to this place?"

"Nurse Ratched," is not as bad as everyone thought she was! Do you know that she has little nurse caps for the children to play with during clinic? Everyone wants to belong to someone."

"Yeah, well while you're in the Christian mood, Mom and Dad are over in the private clinic at Jackson. They want to have dinner after her appointment and they don't want to eat the chicken casserole that we have prepared."

"Why is she here in clinic? What pray tell is the problem, or is it 'my son the doctor syndrome?'"

"Pollyanna, how can you be so cold?! I am telling Jesus what you just said about my sweet, sweet mommy!" Seeing his wife laugh was an energy boost for him. "She has an oval contusion on her right buttock. If she has fallen or unconsciously bumped herself, it is most likely just a bruise."

"Has she been around your brother recently?"

"Yes, they had dinner with them last night, why?"

"Then it's probably a hickey!"

"Mrs. Solberg! You continually surprise me! What about dinner?"

"Whatever pleases your mommy's heart!"

*"Missionary Turns Sarcastic; Dorothy Solberg to Blame,* front page story then? What would *The Miami Herald* give for that? We could use the extra money, Polly!"

A contusion – simple bruise of unknown origin, was the diagnosis of Dorothy's emergency visit to JMH. None too thrilled about the hype her daughter-in law was given by the staff, she was grateful that her son was also held in very high regard. The four Solbergs ate dinner at TGI Fridays, and chatted amicably during the meal. Raymond was amazed at the "serving bowl" portions of the Santa Fe Salad, while Dorothy munched heartily on Chicken Bruschetta over angel hair pasta. Frank and Regina had their TGIF favorite of Jack Daniels baby back ribs with corn on the cob and slaw. Although they were full to the point of the table groaning, the group still managed the devour desserts of Oreo madness and Cracker Jack sundaes.

Dorothy was troubled by this "Pollyanna reputation" that Frank made the mistake of bragging about. She did not like the Solberg name directly mixed with indigents, and certainly didn't want Frank upstaged, even in the early start of his profession.

"Children in the clinic adore Frank," boasted Regina. "The staff at BPEI all think he's pretty wonderful too!"

"Frank does not belong at BPEI doing puppet shows and making an ass of himself, Regina. You need to learn that Miami is not your personal little cruise ship show. You should be nowhere near his work at any time or for any reason."

"Actually, she is not near my work, I am near hers. I'm very proud of Regina and so are a good many of the attending physicians that I will be working under when I do the ophthalmology rotation. She has turned that clinic into an example that all of the departments in JMH need to stand up and take notice of, and believe me, they will."

"What is an attending physician?" The matriarch scowled.

"A faculty member on any given service," Frank enlightened.

"Dad and I are still disappointed to learn that our family name is being thrown around like that."

"Well now it's not that we don't appreciate Regina's compassion; it's the focus of attention on the indigents that we don't like." Indicating his daughter-in-law he added, "We don't mean to squash you, honey, but Frank's image is important even now."

"No problem, Dad, I'm not squashed. It has been said by God, Himself, that those who wish to sing always find a song."

Dorothy raised her eyebrows sharply, "Meaning?"

"Meaning that we love our work, separately and together, and we will continue to sing."

# Chapter Three
## Monique Le Petite

Leaving the restaurant Regina heard the screech of tires on a blue Mustang skid into the parking lot and a loud voice shout, "Now, do it now!" All of a sudden a little brown mixed dog was chucked from the open window onto the pavement, as the car peeled off. Exasperated, the little figure struggled to stand and tried desperately to follow the racing vehicle onto the highway. Regina clasped her hand over her mouth to avoid screaming. Cautiously she entered the parking area and approached the dog. Frank was already by her side as she offered the small animal her takeout. The shaking disoriented dog was now frozen in place, as Frank took her in his arms. Riddled with fleas, her ribs were visible, there was a huge gash on her right ear, and the same eye was swollen shut."

"Well, Pollyanna, it's your call."

"With your permission, Dr. Solberg, I would like to keep her."

"So be it, we'll stop at Wal-Mart for treatments and take her home from there."

Dorothy tried to take control as usual, "If I may interrupt, we should put her in our car and take her to Adam for free."

"No," said Regina, tears streaming down her face, "indigents are our specialty;

Monique comes home with us."

The Solbergs knew when a subject was closed, and did not persist. Both parents kissed the "kids" goodbye and wished them luck with the dog.

"Monique?" asked Frank, "I'm not sure why, but that name seems so fitting."

The little dog settled against Regina wrapped in her light weight sweatshirt for the trip to the store and home. She became known as Monique Le Petite from that point on.

While the rescuers were in Wal-Mart, Monique became frightened and tore at the leather interior of Frank's older model Volvo which was in mint condition. Returning with the supplies, and knowing how Frank venerated his car, Regina was horrified. Given the late hour, she was further shocked by his reaction.

"Well that was bright of us! Of course she is afraid in a strange car. Look what just happened to her? Monique, we are going to count this as our error and we are going to chalk it up to a thing vs. a living thing. Look at the new bed, and toys that your Pollyanna mama has picked out for you."

Monique settled in slowly, and even adjusted to the elevator rides preceding and following her walks. Enjoying the high patio and the view of the Miami River, she played happily with her toys during the long days of work and medical school. Having the basic appearance of a dachshund, Monique definitely had other mixes. Brown and black in color, she was adorable now that her wounds had healed and her personality developed. Description alone had earned her an invitation to the McBride home for a co-celebrated Thanksgiving dinner next week. The festivities were to include the entire McBride crew, Bub and Sis, and the smaller Solberg family.

Before committing to attend, Adam Solberg called to ensure that no gratis services were being solicited on little Monique's behalf.

Holidays have a way of bringing out the sensitivity in all of us, and certainly held true in this setting. Elizabeth and Dorothy argued about which home Regina and Frank would stay in. Frank suggested that they stay with Regina's family this time, as they were hosting the dinner, and at the Solberg house over Christmas, where the favor would be reciprocated. Considering this would be Monique's first experience away from her new home, and adding the menagerie at the Solberg house, Regina agreed with her husband. Dorothy and Raymond were nice enough people, but their inability to mind their own business also factored into the choice. Neither stay would be lengthy anyway, due to their work schedules and Frank's study load.

The holiday planning was distracted by a telephone call from Jeannie Nugent.

"Regina, can I come down for awhile? I have to talk to you."

"Jeannie, are you crying? What's the matter, honey? Of course, come right down. Yes, Frank is home and you are certainly not interrupting a thing."

Answering the door, Frank was shaken by the condition of their friend.

Jeannie walked into the living room, picked Monique up, and burst into a new set of tears.

"It's Chuck," she sobbed. "Elena Garcia, the ward clerk, from West Wing, is infatuated with him. I tried not to let it upset me, but she is calling frequently with intermittent aches and pains. I just found out that her uncle, Miguel Garcia, lives in this building and has a gorgeous boat docked right here by our apartments. She had the nerve to bring cookies to work for Chuck yesterday, which he brought down to me. The card hidden inside did not say to Chuck and Jeannie, it said to CHUCK."

"Jeannie, Chuck is aware of Elena's crush on him, and he is not one bit entertained by it. Her father, Jorge Garcia, is an attending on the Nephrology Service. Have you spoken to Chuck about your concerns?" he asked gently.

"No, I didn't want to appear childish and jealous, but I have found myself trying to spy on her, and I am constantly distracted at work."

"Well I would certainly think that Chuck will tactfully put a stop to her calls now, regardless of who her father is. How old is she?" Regina asked with concern in her voice.

"Nineteen, and in pre-med classes at night; that will be her next excuse to call him."

"Regina, as a woman in a similar role as Jeannie's; what is your position?" Frank glanced at his wife.

"I would start by speaking to my husband since he has already told Frank that he doesn't find this nonsense cute. He probably didn't realize that you are aware of the situation and didn't want to upset you. Is she calling your home or his pager?"

"Both."

"Frank, would you talk to Chuck? Jeannie, would you mind if he did?"

"I wouldn't mind at all, they're like brothers."

"Do you want Chuck to know that you were here?" Frank asked.

"Yes, I want everything out in the open."

"We have anatomy lab late tomorrow afternoon. After that I'll invite him back here for burgers. Can you two ladies can ride home together?"

"Beyond the shadow of a doubt," Jeannie was already relieved.

Frank and Chuck had seen Elena hanging around the ground floor café. They had also noticed on multiple occasions that she *just happened* to be in the vicinity of the elevator when they arrived home from classes. Chuck showed no interest that Frank had ever witnessed, but this lady was on the chase, and there was no doubt about it.

Dan McBride and his partner were scheduled to have a meeting in Miami that afternoon, and stopped by BPEI to see Regina. He was very proud of his stepdaughter, and favored her over all eight of the children. Nurse McNeal was charmed upon being introduced, and graciously accepted his offer to build storage shelves so that Regina did not have to haul the bulk of her supplies back and forth every morning. Administration was called to the clinic, in true military efficiency, and a closet with a sturdy lock was assigned for the supplies.

The building materials and labor would be donated by Dan and his associate, Lamar Mac Michaels, a quiet man who was recently widowed. Construction would begin the Monday after Thanksgiving.

While in town Dan and Lamar took Frank and Regina to dinner at Shorty's Bar-B-Que; where they thoroughly enjoyed hearing about their work. Regina loved her stepfather and so did Frank. Charming and sophisticated, he was a barrel of fun and only if solicited, a resource of helpful advice. Ending too quickly, the evening was like a shot in the arm for the newly married Solbergs.

The next night Chuck and Jeannie were over for dinner. They had swiftly sorted out the problem with Elena Garcia and hoped to hear no more from her. Elena was a dark skinned Cuban, who wore enough perfume, makeup, and jewelry to be a walking mall. She had long straight black hair which she usually wore parted in the middle and hanging. Claiming that she didn't realize that Chuck was married, she flirtatiously apologized, and purring good-bye, returned to her computer. Regina was not sure this would be the last of her, and neither was Jeannie.

The Nugents were going to Chuck's parents for Thanksgiving and Jeannie's for the Christmas break. The Pot Luck Club would have their own celebrations prior to each holiday. Thanksgiving was at Nugent's place and Christmas had been scheduled for the Solberg's.

The Turkey was the group's expense and the wives brought

all of the trimmings. Regina made a sweet potato casserole and was at Jeannie's early to help set up. Typically, the evening was a blast. Everyone ate and compared family gripes related to out of town visits.  Offers to keep Monique were plentiful from Miami residents, but Regina would not leave her. The Nugents had three Siamese cats which were free fed and could be left home alone, while various pets of the other medical students were placed for the holiday among each other. Overall, the group had to admit that while traveling was taxing, it was both welcomed and necessary!

After the break, it was business as usual. Frank returned to his studies, and Regina to her clinic work. M&M Architects, Dan McBride and Lamar Mac Michaels appeared bright and early at BPEI to begin construction. The Administrator, Paul Newhart, appeared to present Regina with her new promotion as Outpatient Clinic Coordinator; while Dan and Lamar took turns hugging her, and her co-workers applauded.

Lamar Mac Michaels inquired about any other medical protocol in addition to the fire regulations regarding the closet, and was referred to Nurse McNeal.

"Apologies, Ma'am, I did not get your first name." In the past the response to this statement would have been a snappy, "Nurse!" Today however, it was a soft spoken, pleasant, "Frances."

"I'm Lamar Mac Michaels, a pleasure to meet you. May I call you Frances?"

"To be sure, and the pleasure is mine, Lamar. We appreciate your time and materials in this project, and we also appreciate your own Regina."

"Are there any other restrictions we should know about besides the ordinary building codes?"

"Not that I am aware of. The closet will remain locked and does not block any areas of egress. We are not storing any questionable materials, so I think we're fine."

"Very well, then, I'm holding you responsible, Nurse Frances."

Regina and Dan exchanged sparkling glances. Both noted the slight coloring of Nurse McNeal's face, not to mention the wide smile on Lamar's.

Regina signed the next patient in and offered him the usual turkey salad sandwich with all of the "ghetto trimmings." Delighted with the hospitality, he complimented the cook and the lemonade. He stated his name, Irving Berlin, and continued to give Regina his history. Regina was a former dancer, not a musician, and made no connection. Glancing at the door she saw Dan, Lamar, Nurse McNeal, and Frank, who had stopped by for lunch, gazing into the room aghast! Right behind them rushed Susan Greer, the head of Public Relations.

"Mr. Berlin, I am so sorry! You are scheduled as a VIP patient in the Private Clinic upstairs. I don't know how you wound up here, but we will certainly research this error."

Mr. Berlin beamed, and indicating Regina, he responded, "Well, I asked this adorable red head if I might see a doctor, and she immediately provided me with a clipboard, pen, and a plate of delicious food. I recognized her at once as one of the entertainers on the MS Sonafjord, when we took our Mediterranean cruise several years ago. She did not recognize me, but I have enjoyed talking to her so much, that I never even thought that I might be in the wrong clinic." Regina turned red and looked puzzled. Frank winked at her from the doorway and asked if she was familiar with the song, *White Christmas*. Irving Berlin stood up and bowing, kissed her hand. Regina looked at the floor realizing that none of the tiles would have space enough to crawl under. She managed to graciously ease her way out of the situation with everyone's admiration.

Without further ado, the closet was transformed into a space efficient storage area. Once again the M&M crew treated the "kids" to dinner, but this time they invited Nurse Frances McNeal!

"Oh I couldn't she gushed. I don't even have a change of clothes."

"Oh please come," Regina begged, "I'm wearing my uniform too, and they're in work clothes as well."

The dinner was at the Melody Inn, which was a lovely French restaurant. Everyone had a wonderful time and Regina thought she had never seen Frances look so lovely. She was radiant with her hair falling loosely about her shoulders. Lamar had taken her arm and seated her beside him, which flattered her immensely.

# Chapter Four
# Early Recognition

Frank Solberg lifted his freezer chilled glass and swallowed the last of his orange juice. Regina always had a lovely breakfast going along with the clinic goodies.

Complimenting her eggs-in-a-basket and ham, he pulled her into his lap and kissed her. "I have an appointment with the head of the hand service in Orthopedics this morning. They are looking in advance for summer help and the experience would be wonderful. We could also use the extra cash."

Orthopedics was the field in which Frank wanted to specialize, and he was already aware of the competition involved. "Well I'm sure they will recognize expertise when they see it. Just don't let them mess with our beach time, honey, JMH loves to make medical students their slaves. They are booking second year students to do histories and physicals for the summer as well, and Jeannie has already cautioned Chuck not to sign up for an open deal."

Chuck was looking toward Internal Medicine for his post

graduate field. Following a year of book diving, the medical students were all anxious to try out their required doctor's bags!

Christmas was almost upon them, sparking a Chinese take-out dinner at the Solbergs,' where Regina and Jeannie were busy finishing up their homemade gifts for the both families. Plaster of Paris ornaments lined a card table for boxing and wrapping. The unexpected cold snap was a bonus that further enhanced holiday moods. Jeannie held up one of the miniature gingerbread men and commented that the ornaments looked good enough to eat. Both couples had decorated their own trees in the crafts and decided that their early fall start was none too soon.

Chuck was delighted that he'd been hired for the upcoming summer to do histories and physicals on admitted patients at $25.00 a piece.

Frank had been enlightened that afternoon that the hand service hours were strictly volunteer, and a privilege to the lucky slave who might be selected to work them. He mentioned his own intent to indulge in the fortune that Chuck and many of their friends would be taking part in.

Later that night silvery lightning streaked the blackened sky followed by thunder that shook the tall buildings of the Isla Del Mar. The boats in the Miami River rocked and rattled the docks in protest, while palm trees bent with the wind. Monique was terrified and found comfort under the covers of Regina's side of the king sized bed, as the sleepy couple donned their night clothes.

Recalling the conversation at dinner, Regina addressed her concerns.

"I know that twenty-five bucks a patient sounds like a great deal, but in the great scheme of things, it really isn't."

"Explain yourself, Pollyanna!" Frank held up an empty roll of Christmas wrap, as a sword. Regina grabbed a pillow to ward off the blow and continued, "The Hand Service here is known throughout the world, and the Chairman, Dr. Leo Gerehauser, is in France as we speak for six months with Dr. Jacque Pilet. They will return together and Dr. Pilet will stay here for six months encompassing the summer. From what I understand, this man creates life like prosthetics for patients who have suffered partial or total hand losses. The experience is far more valuable than $25.00 here or there and would serve as a great asset on your application for an orthopedic residency."

The pirate poser continued in a crude British accent, "So let me ascertain that I understand you correctly, wench. I am supposed to soldier on to a nice little summer seminar making no money at all, while my wife works herself to death and forfeits the extras that the other wives will be enjoying. Is that really fair, Regina?"

"Aye, matey, while I appreciate your saintly personification, my intentions are not quite so pure! We are looking toward the big picture, Frank, and we are doing fine on the booty from BPEI. Opportunities like this come along once every blue moon, and due to a lack of foresight, the real treasure could slip away. Accepting an invitation to work with the best of the best, in your highly competitive field, would serve far better than insulting the big wigs by snubbing the chance for a few extra doubloons now."

"Well let's see if I am invited before we worry about it. In the meantime, I should apply for the H&P's so that I don't miss out on the chances there."

"Once you apply and get accepted, can you back out? There are only so many hours in the day."

"No, that would definitely be frowned upon."

Monique had come out from under cover and was observing the pirates with her head cocked to the side. Listening to the raging storm, the buccaneers were glad that they were not really on a pirate ship. Laughing they held each other gently and drifted off to sleep.

The following morning, the acting head of the Hand Service notified Frank that they were very impressed with his credentials. Having worked as an ambulance attendant for several years before medical school, and in the emergency room as well, he was a prime candidate. They asked him to observe and assist in surgery that evening.

Demonstrating excellent technique, immediate pick up skills, and gifted agility with the surgical instruments, the vote was unanimous. Solberg was the first choice and would be a definite asset to the hand service.

Arriving home late, Regina had his dinner waiting. "Well, how did it go?"

"I have been accepted as the lucky slave, but I don't know if I want the position."

"When do they want an answer?"

"My response must be in by tomorrow afternoon, and actually, they were annoyed by my hesitation, and reminded me that several third and fourth years are waiting in line for this opportunity. The Chief Resident, Dr. Ann Garfield, is an absolute snob."

"Speaking of snobs, your parents called, and they are waiting up to hear from you. And you thought things couldn't get any worse!"

"Pollyanna, your name suits you. How is it that you can make me laugh no matter what?"

The Solbergs were awake, and waiting with bated breath to hear the outcome. Setting dinner out, Regina heard Frank's answers.

"Yes, yes they did. No, not yet, I want to sleep on it. No, Regina feels the same ways as you guys do, did she not tell you that? Yes, she is one in a million. Sure she's awake, my dinner is waiting. Spaghetti, meatballs, salad, garlic bread and chocolate whipped cream cake. You too. I will, I will."

"Must I repeat the whole dialogue?"

"Spare me."

The younger Solbergs ate their dinner on the patio by candlelight. Monique joined in the feast, lifting her little nose high in the air to assess the breeze from the river.

Stopping by the next day for lunch at Pollyanna's, he found her busy with an anxious patient. Frances came over to him immediately, as she had become very fond of Frank, and loved Regina.

"Since Pollyanna is temporarily detained, may I fix your lunch?"

"I wouldn't dream of having you do that, I'll fix it myself."

"Too late," she handed him the plate of last night's leftovers which, expecting him, his wife had already heated in the microwave.

Frances noticed his pensive expression, but tried not to pry.

"Regina will be out any minute, Coke or lemonade?"

"Coke, please. Thanks so much."

Frances could stand it no longer. "Did you know that an RN as old as I am has an automatic license to meddle? The catch is that it is only valid when someone they love is involved, and I love you and Regina."

"Is that a warning that you are going to meddle?" Frank grinned.

"No, it is just an introduction. She's right, you know? Regina is right, Frank; I'm the one who told her about the Hand Service, and I must agree that turning down a chance to work with them would be a big mistake."

"What about Regina? Where does she figure in?"

Taking the chair next to him, she continued. "Frank I never thought I would say this, but she is being advised by God, Himself! Sometimes when I see her, I just know she is praying, and I envy her. She covers her depth with a very enjoyable sarcasm, but the depth is still there. I think she converts more people than the churches do by the way she practices her faith. She lives it!"

"Nothing seems to rattle or concern her, and that scares me," Frank twirled his spaghetti.

"I know what you mean. She takes everything in stride, letting a lot of petty stuff roll right off her back. The other day an obnoxious faculty member was flirting with her and remarked, 'When you smile, your whole face lights up.' Regina pleasantly responded,

'Well if only half lights up, please be sure to let me know, it means I've had a stroke.' Attending in charge or not, Regina abruptly put him right in his place and never missed a skip."

"I still worry about her."

"Trust me, Doctor, she's no martyr! If she is backing this position it is because of good solid sense. Listen to her, Frank."

Frank stood up and kissed Frances on the cheek as Regina walked up to them.

"The wife is always the last to know," she laughed.

"Never mind, wench, tell me about your face lighting up!"

"Oh, he's harmless. He thinks the world awaits him."

"What's his name?"

"No clue, matey."

"Frances, who is he?" Frank persisted.

"His name is Dr. Alan Boyd, he is married and has a set of twins. He also knows that Regina is a one man woman, as she made that perfectly clear!"

# Chapter Five
# Litter Box Luau

Regina turned on the oven and started setting the table for the Pot Luck Christmas dinner. The main course was Lasagna which had been prepared earlier. Everyone from out of town would leave for the Christmas break in the morning, carrying bitter-sweet emotions about saying good-bye to Miami, even for a few days.

Chuck had cued Regina that he was planning to slip out briefly to pick up a Christmas surprise for Jeannie. Mike Reynolds, the Chief Resident on the Internal Medicine Service, had ordered a pearl necklace for his mother. The matching earrings were not needed, as his mother already had some. Being in the right place at the right time had enabled Chuck to buy them at a very discounted price. Mayors Jewelers had just gotten the set of pearls in, and Mike was to pick up the jewelry tonight and bring Chuck his half of the gift.

Across the city, Elena Garcia was also busy finishing her plans to set up and serve a small Hawaiian spread on her uncle's boat at Isla Del Mar. Previously getting wind of Jeannie's earrings and the drop off plans, she wasted no time scheming. Elena offered the unsuspecting Chief Resident her services, stating that she had overheard his conversation, and was going to the mall herself this evening and then to her uncle's at Isla Del Mar. She would be delighted to pick up his packages and deliver the one where ever it belonged there, taking the other part to work the next morning and passing it to Mike during rounds.

"What's his name again?" she meowed.

"Chuck Nugent, I think he may live in the same building as your uncle."

"Do you know his pager number?"

"Of Course, I'll write it down for you. Are you sure this isn't an inconvenience?"

"Not at all! Why should both of us run? It's ironic that things worked out so that I can be of assistance to you, Mike. You work too hard to have any extra errands!"

"Well, I owe you big! Just page Chuck and he will come down to the lobby to get the smaller box. He'll be home for sure, because they have their pot luck dinner tonight and he knows to sneak down to the lobby upon my signal. Gosh, Elena, now I can switch call for tonight and get out of here after rounds tomorrow! Like I said, I owe you big!"

"No problem at all, Mike, I promise."

Humming a little song, Elena tenderly arranged the platter to ensure that flaming center would complement the bacon wrapped water chestnuts and stuffed banana leaves. Two additional small trays of canopies and delicately filled puff pastry shells also stood ready for the trap. The gift wrapped earrings would be hidden on her uncle's boat, where she could innocently present them to Chuck staging a light singe of her wrist in the process. The rest would all be downhill, and the flawless plan delighted her!

Regina stepped out on the balcony to set up the rest of the chairs. From the corner of her eye, she thought she saw Elena walking on the dock. Slipping into the master bedroom, she tried to get a better look from the sliding glass doors. Grabbing the cordless phone she dialed Jeannie, "Elena Garcia is setting up a nice little spread of some kind on the upper deck of her fat uncle's boat."

"I'll be right down."

Past experiences had made Regina incredibly street -smart, and she didn't like the looks of this one bit. "Father, please protect my friends, and let this setting be completely unrelated to the Nugents."

Her next call was to Chuck. "Tell me who is bringing the gift tonight and where, so that I can plan to distract Jeannie."

"Mike Reynolds will page me and I will meet him in the lobby. I need you to send me to the eat-in café for ice."

Interference was not Regina's practice, but these were her friends, and according to Frances, Elena had already destroyed two marriages at JMH, one of which resulted in a suicide. The press had been discreetly distracted to protect Jorge Garcia's famous name.

Calling the hospital Regina learned that Mike Reynolds had switched his schedule to be on call tonight, so that he could leave Miami in the morning.

Jeannie arrived and gasped at the view of the boat, as tears stung her eyes.

"She isn't going to stop, Regina. Why is she here?"

"We don't know that yet, but have you cleaned your litter box recently?"

"I'll do it in the morning before we leave. Why, does it smell bad?"

"I certainly hope so."

"Has Chuck complained about it?"

"No."

"What in the world are you up to Regina?"

"Hopefully, nothing."

Guests arrived and to Regina's delight, the dinner started with more hands than needed. Chuck's pager went off and Regina sent him downstairs for ice as planned. Jeannie looked shocked, but said nothing. Watching from the bedroom, and oblivious to their guests, the two girls saw Elena leave the boat and head in the direction of the lobby. They slipped upstairs to Jeannie's and dragging a very full litter box, crouched down on the corner of her balcony.

"Wait for the signal," Regina counseled, "we must be absolutely sure."

Frances stepped out of the café and phoned Jeannie's place.

"Here they come! Chuck was mortified to see Elena and she just advised him that the package is on her uncle's boat for safety. Get her girls!"

Without further delay, the litter pan was emptied over the

balcony, its' contents gushing down like a smelly volcano and covering the luau. The girls immediately stepped inside and took the stairs back down to the pot luck dinner.

Frances joined them, laughing hysterically. She had watched as Chuck and Elena boarded the boat and could restrain herself no longer. Tears ran down her face as she described Elena's expression and Chuck's uncontrollable laughter once he had secured his package. Elena was furious and tried to slap him across the face, but he moved out of her reach too quickly.

Frances hugged both girls and raised her eyes to heaven. "Father, Regina was right, You are a barrel of fun! Please advise what we need to do, if anything, to right whatever we can here. Please forgive our little prank, Lord, and help Elena to find a man of her own!"

Regina followed, "Father, I'll talk to You more about this later, and I know that I'm probably in deep trouble! I am ready to make this up to You in whatever You call on me to do." Winking, she added, "I love You more than life itself, Abba, but it was fun. My only regret would be if we displeased You."

Light rain began to fall causing the chairs on the balcony to be moved in slightly to the covered patio, but also entertaining the Pot Luck Club with a panicked shout of language that would make a sailor put soap in his mouth. The litter box contents were now getting wet, and would leave tell tale signs and odors on Uncle Miguel's pride and joy.

While the guests dwindled, Frances helped Regina and

Jeannie clean up the kitchen. Frank and Chuck, both sporting amused yet puzzled expressions were talking.

"Frances is like a second mother to Regina," Chuck commented munching on a anise cookie.

"Frances is a wonderful lady, and is dating her stepfather's partner."

"Regina and Jeannie are also like sisters, and I think they know something about what happened on Garcia's boat tonight. All three of them look guilty to me, let's have some fun," Chuck yawned in spite of the coffee he had consumed.

"Girls, I present the Honorable Judge Charles Nugent, who demands to know what involvement you had in the decorating of the Garcia vessel."

It was Frances who answered, "Well Judge, I believe that in this sovereign nation, we are innocent until proven guilty."

"Fine, but do you guys know that if any of you were on that boat, you were trespassing?" The unrobed judge laughed.

"Your Honor, none of us were anywhere near that boat," Frances defended.

Frank was leaning against the wall with a second plate of Sicilian Trifle, "O.K. spill it, you three. We know that you were involved."

"What makes you so certain?" Regina loved a challenge.

"Jeannie, why are you so quiet?" the mock judge continued.

"I have the right to an attorney."

Frances suggested that everyone have a cup of coffee and placed another plate of anise cookies on the table. Omitting the detail of Jeannie's Christmas surprise, the events of the evening were explained. Frances, who did not believe in gossip, spoke quietly to the four younger people.

"It is my understanding that Elena Garcia has a history of pursuing married men.

Although she is only nineteen, two marriages have been destroyed in relation to her interference with the husbands involved. While no person other than the one who took their own life, can be blamed for a suicide, the cause of it definitely holds evidence. This was the result of the second incident. Dr. Jorge Garcia, Elena's father and a famous nephrology attending, was frantic. *The Miami Herald* did not mention his daughter in the article, but the escape was too narrow for the Risk Management Department. If they get wind of the incident tonight, Elena could face dismissal. Her father had placed her in therapy but I don't know if she stills continues her treatment."

Chuck slowly shook his head, "The problem is that she places herself in positions that have the potential to destroy the reputations of innocent people.

I don't know the legalities involved since her uncle lives here, but I think we need to get a restraining order."

Frances stirred her coffee, "You could get a restraining order, Chuck, keeping her a certain distance from you, but remember that she works at JMH.

That alone will carry complications. This situation tonight could have been very ugly, which is why Regina intervened and I assisted her."

"So what options do we have?" Frank sounded concerned.

Indicating Chuck, Frances answered, "Your Honor, since I have already disclosed my license to meddle to Dr. Solberg, I would be happy to approach Risk Management quietly, and let them know that we have another potential problem."

"Could you three be charged with trespassing?" Frank was still uneasy.

"Nobody trespassed," Regina answered reassuringly.

"That's correct," reassured Frances, "and moreover, there are ten stories in this building and I doubt that the Garcias will pursue feline searches or cat litter testing, which wouldn't prove anything anyway. They're also smart enough to realize that even in the worst case scenario, given Elena's history, a court would find that she got her just dessert. The newspapers would also enjoy   entertaining stories like this one, and nobody wants that kind of publicity."

The two couples agreed that Frances should talk to Risk Management and call the Nugents in if necessary. They were also concerned about a revenge issue, given Elena's unsuccessful attempt tonight.

Regina called Patrick Dain, her family's rector, and told him what had happened. Although he was laughing, he did caution Regina that she must be careful when taking matters into her own hands. He couldn't help adding that he agreed that Elena definitely needed to be stopped, and that he would personally pray that this lady would be blessed with self restraint in the future.

Frances was glowing as she told Regina that Lamar had surprised her with tickets for a Christmas Cruise. Regina, having been very instrumental in the arrangements, enjoyed her excitement, and helped her pack. The two women embraced and said good-bye for the holidays.

Christmas for Frank and Regina, was filled with joy. They stayed at the Solbergs, but both families went back and forth to each other's homes, and everyone got along beautifully. Dorothy and Raymond admired their daughter-in-law, even though they could not control her, and Dan and Elizabeth loved Frank. Dorothy noted that the "kids" were glowing and therefore must be very happy. The Mc Brides were also moved by the obvious love that Frank and Regina had for each other, and little Monique was " in like Flynn," in both houses and enjoyed the constant flow of attention.

Christmas was one of Regina's favorite times of the year, as she loved the Nativity. She missed her own display of imported Italian resin figures expertly painted and housed in the beautiful stable that Frank and his father had made for her. The set was up the day after Thanksgiving and would remain in place until after the New Year. Each morning Regina would sit by the manger with a cup of coffee and marvel at it. Every night the tiny blue lights surrounding the stable sparkled in the living room, bidding great tidings through the full length glass patio doors, to the boats docked in the Miami River. Both her parents and the Solbergs had nice Nativity scenes as well, and she enjoyed sitting by them every chance she could.

Holiday food was everywhere including cakes, cookies,

Christmas candy, gingerbread houses, kringles, strudels, fruit, nuts, cheese platters, cold cut platters, mini rolls, pita chips, and every kind of dip and spread imaginable. The houses smelled of pine branches and cranberries intermingled with cinnamon and baked apples.

Early in December Frank had gone to the University of Miami Wood Shop and made a number 1 from a little piece of walnut that they found in the U-haul that had moved them to Miami. Regina had picked it up and said, "This must have broken off someone's piece of furniture." After calling U-Haul and letting the desk know about it, they had never heard back.

"Well it's too sentimental to throw away, so I'll stick it in the doll cabinet and someday, we'll find a use for it." Frank polished the #1, fastened a metal loop to the top, and placed an ornament hook through it. Regina was thrilled to tears, and cherished it more than any of the other presents she received.

It symbolized not only their first Christmas together, but Frank's complete understanding of her. The ornament also took a good deal of time and effort to make. Frank could not resist the chance to tease her, so addressing Dan, he said, "I may as well return the gorgeous bracelet I brought her, before it winds up in a garage sale." Blushing, Regina held up her wrist to show off the beautiful bangle.

All too soon the year came to an end with a big celebration at the country club where both families played golf. Midnight exchanges revealed two very different families who had accepted each other through the marriage of their children. Raymond asked Regina what is was like to be a Solberg in 1980, while Marge kept her own thoughts to herself. Regina smiled at her husband and answered, "I believe that it is unfair for any one person to have as much joy as I do, but I am grateful to God, and honored to be Mrs. Frank Solberg."

Dorothy, obviously not planning to leave well enough alone this year either, asked, "Marge, how do you feel about being a Solberg?" Marge, tipping her fourth glass of eggnog slurred, "Whatever."

Dan and Regina smiled at each other, as they had talked frequently about the adjustments of marriage and acceptance of the families.

# Chapter Six
# The Mockingbird

Hectic schedules resumed as issues that had considerately slept under the blanket of holiday joy, stretched, yawned, and resurfaced. Such was the case with an injustice that would sadden America all the way to the history books.

Former United States Marine and military police officer, Arthur McDuffie, had been brutally beaten by four police officers on December 17th of last year. McDuffie was driving a 1973 black and orange Kawasaki motorcycle with a suspended license and accumulated traffic citations. The tragedy began with another traffic violation leading to an eight minute chase and ending with a horrific and brutal assault that resulted in the victim's death four days later.

The community was outraged and Regina remembered hearing the sirens and commotion, followed by comments the next morning in the elevator. Two faculty members were exasperated, "Four white police officers beat the holy hell out a black man last night after he surrendered to their chase! They pulled his helmet off and cracked his skull with their night sticks. He's in critical condition, and thanks to their stupidity, so is this environment."

Medical staffs throughout the city were stunned. The general consensus of opinion was that black, white, or sky blue pink, justice is justice. Police officers had a dangerous calling beyond the shadow of a doubt, but deliberate brutality was never taken lightly. Miami of all places was already a racial time bomb waiting for a detonator.

The officers involved, suspended by the end of December, were just recently fired. Due to the volatile atmosphere, the trial was shifted to Tampa, where jury selection began on March 31, 1980 and concluded with "an all- white, all-male jury."

Tension in the air could be cut with a hacksaw as citizens moved through the days clinging to the hope that all would be well. Even though friends of both races seemed to agree that the incident was appalling and should be brought to justice, the words "black and white" tossed about restlessly in most conversations.

Regina, having been born and raised in New York, never did understand racial distinctions. She felt that different colors of skin were beautiful and that all men were loved equally in the eyes of God, but Frank still worried night and day about the effect this would have on her.

Finally in mid May, the verdict acquitting all of the officers involved, after less than three hours of jury deliberation, sent outraged Miami residents pouring into the streets. Downtown at the Metro Justice Building 5000 attended a protest which by 6:00 pm had turned into a full blown riot with 3 dead and 23 injured, many of them critically. Cars were upturned and ignited, rocks were thrown into the windows of the Justice Building, and intervening police officers were being assaulted. Angry screaming and gun fire could be heard for blocks, drowned out only by emergency vehicles.

The Nugents and the Solbergs watched the downtown fires from their balconies, as panic and fear infiltrated the buildings of Isla Del Mar.

Cuban residents brought out their guns and loud, angry communications were exchanged all over the complex in Spanish. Women and children were crying in fright while they clung to each other in the elevators.

Despite National Guardsmen pouring into the city, by the next day, 165 people were injured and 12 more were killed as violence spread. Sniper fire, burglaries, and looting were checked by an 8:00 pm to 6:00 am curfew and a temporary ban on the sale of firearms and liquor.

Arthur McDuffie's mother appeared on television begging people to stop the violence. Regina fell to her knees as she had many times since December 17th the preceding year. "Father, please make me an instrument of Your peace in this horrible situation. I submit my application now, and I beg You to consider me.

I am from the Bronx, You know! Let me assist in any way that You will allow me to, and please protect all who are fighting to end this war in our streets."

Frank and Chuck, escorted by the National Guard, were stuck at the hospital while Regina and Jeannie stayed together. Officials temporarily raised one of the bridges to contain the violence and to attempt to keep those Cubans and Haitians, who were currently uninvolved, from joining in the war.

Heavy scents of gasoline and dark smoke clouds hung in the air, announcing the terror. Faces expressed fear and anger, while the sirens blared and helicopters frequented the sky. The media flashed pictures of the understaffed hospital complex and the exhausted personnel stranded there. Stretchers carrying bleeding patients were crowded in the halls, as clerical staff tried desperately to control the hysterical relatives of the wounded.

Despite the ominous surroundings, Regina was going to work the next morning come hell or high water. Armed with a long sock filled with a paper weight and change, she was prepared to sling the weapon if necessary. Cubans, Haitians, Whites, Blacks, or Aliens, she was going to the clinic.

Although even the palm trees appeared to shout their warning, the streets were ghostly quiet. Signs of caution were everywhere, but so were the National Guards, and Regina, so far, was not afraid. Continuing her path from the parking garage through the long alley, Regina stayed alert. After a few minutes she saw the large man approaching. The size of a small mountain, he was moving swiftly toward her. Petrified, she called for backup, "Father, please stay with me! I am afraid."

Shaking, Regina threw her purse down, assumed a solid stance, and wrapped the sock around her hand.

The man picked up her purse, and Regina spoke, "You may have my purse, sir, but please understand that I am here to assist anyone who needs me. I hold no prejudice and I am in Good Company."

"I may be a black man, but I hold no prejudice either." Handing Regina her purse he smiled, stepping back quickly as he observed her weapon.

"Well I didn't say you did," Regina faked relaxation.

"What's in the sock?"

"Lunch money!"

Both alley occupants laughed nervously.

"Where are you headed, ma'am?"

"Bascom Palmer," she responded, extending her still quivering hand, "Regina Solberg."

"Wyatt Clements, may I escort you? I figure it will keep my brothers safe from your sock."

Regina folded the sock in embarrassment and shoved it in her purse, as Wyatt took the weighted satchel for the journey.

Arriving at the steps of BPEI, they were met at once by two armed National Guards, one "black" and one "white." They cautiously eyed Wyatt, who was still carrying Regina's purse."

Regina turned to Wyatt and kissed him gently on the cheek, while tears filled his eyes. The bewildered guardsmen exchanged glances when Wyatt, handing Regina her purse, responded, "For future information, Regina, never show a weapon in a setting like this again, even if it is just a sock."

Accompanied by an escort, Frank and Chuck burst through the door, and Regina introduced her new acquaintance.

"Frank, this is Wyatt Clements, Mr. Clements, my husband, Frank Solberg."

"Chuck Nugent," he stepped forward extending his hand.

Frank hugged and kissed his wife advising her not to interpret his action as  approval for her departure from the safety of Isla Del Mar. Chuck walked to the desk to call Jeannie letting her know that Regina was safe, and without further conversation the entire group dispersed to their positions.

Frances McNeal rushed to Regina and hugged her, "You scared the daylights out of us. Mind you, - you didn't surprise us!"

"Reporting for duty, ma'am."

"Good, we need you, Solberg! We're having orientation for a new resident transferring in from Chicago this morning. He just had to run back to his car for his pager."

"He'll probably run back to his plane when he sees the military dotting our streets."

The elevator door opened. "Oh Doctor Clements, may I introduce our Clinic Coordinator, Regina Solberg."

"A pleasure Mrs. Solberg," they shook hands for the second time that morning.

Weeks passed and wounds slowly healed as the Miami population had hoped. Many were still skittish but life eventually went on as usual and sirens were once again merely part of the hospital's music.

Wyatt and Sylvia Clements lived at the Doral and quickly became friends with the Nugents and the Solbergs. Sylvia was a tall and graceful Jamaican lady who loved style and worked at as a court reporter.

Lamar Mac Michaels frequently visited Miami to see Frances and at the same time to transport care packages from Frank and Regina's parents. Arriving late in the afternoon, he brought two large boxes of emergency supplies. "We were all worried sick about you kids, and I was ready to kidnap Frances and take her out of here!"

Frances nodded toward Regina, "She's even more stubborn than I am. She was out walking through the alley during the worst of it!"

Regina responded, "Of course there's no need to share that information with your partner, sir."

"Young lady, it's too late! Your husband already told him. Of course he waited until the after we knew that you were safe."

"Well why don't you and Frances join us for dinner?"

"Too late again! Frances and I have already arranged for you kids, the Nugents, and the Clements to join us at The Rustic Inn Crab House," Lamar grinned.

Arriving at the restaurant, they saw a car displaying multiple Karate stickers blocking the driveway. Their caravan of three vehicles extended into the highway, while the owner of the obstacle strutted across the parking lot in his black belted uniform to flag a friend. The Solbergs and the Nugents were the first car in line. Regina stepped out of the passenger side and asked the driver to please move his car so the three of their vehicles might be able to get out of the way. Turning, he shot Regina an irritated glance, slowly walked to his vehicle, and finally exited the restaurant parking lot. Frank and Chuck were beside themselves, while Regina and Jeannie remained calm. As they were seated, a visibly rattled Frank asked, "Pollyanna, did you think it wise to taunt the professional butt kicker?"

Jeannie answered, "Who taunted him? He was blocking the driveway. Karate teacher or not, he was causing a potential accident, showing off his little black belt."

"Jeannie, have you already forgotten the violence we have all just lived through," Chuck was as shaken as Frank was.

Frances chimed in, "He was white, wasn't he?"

Wyatt could not resist the chance, "Frank you need to confiscate that sock!"

Sylvia feeling left out demanded to know what sock her husband just made reference to, while Lamar figured he may as well jump in too. "I think it is clear that women sometimes don't recognize danger, while men are basically ..."

"Chickens," Regina and Jeannie interrupted simultaneously.

Large buckets of garlic crabs and wooden mallets lined the table, while the  extensive raw bar buffet beckoned from the wall, offering cherry stone clams, oysters, and shrimp. Deep dish salads and fresh baked rolls complimented the meal, along with large jar glasses of sweet tea. The evening was filled with laughter and sighs of relief that the nightmare had finally come to an end. Frances and Lamar thoroughly enjoyed the three younger couples and the reverse.

Sylvia remarked smiling, "You three girls are pistols! I need to take lessons from you."

"They're not pistols," Lamar corrected, "they're scud missiles, and we'll be needing you to be the rational one in the group, if you don't mind!"

The four gentlemen raised their glasses, egging each other on, while their women rolled their eyes and laughed.

# Chapter Seven
# Face in the Window

The summer heat accompanied by the humidity, was unbearable. Monique sought refuge in her little pool on the patio and happily played in the shaded area of the balcony when she decided to stay dry. Frank and Regina would rise early on weekends for a trip to the beach before it got too hot, as apple boarding was a sport they never seemed to grow tired of. Supplied with a cooler containing their breakfast, they were among the first to hit the causeway hoping to ride the shoreline as the seagulls cheered them on.

Saturday or Sunday afternoons were usually reserved for the pool at Isla Del Mar or over at the Doral where Wyatt and Sylvia lived. Cook outs were economically appropriate fun for the "six pack," and beat the daylights out of running the oven in the hundred degree temperatures. Wyatt and Sylvia had come over last night to show off their new puppy, a rescued cocker spaniel mix named Clementine. When they explained the horrific conditions she came from, Chuck and Jeannie toyed with the idea of taking one of her littermates.

Regina was tossing bacon bits into the potato salad when Frank answered the door. Jeannie entered carrying a little ball of fluff with a big personality. Artful Dodger, to be called Dodger, had swiped Chuck's wallet during their introduction at the shelter. He was Clementine's brother and the last of the litter due to a mild deformity in one of his legs. Jeannie had begged the shelter attendant not to euthanize the puppy, and won after a mild debate, when he was adopted by the Nugents. Frank immediately tapped the little leg into place and the puppy was already walking better. While the six pack had their get together this afternoon, Monique would have a party of her own!

The couples chatted easily as the boys cooked burgers and the girls set up the trimmings. Sylvia shared concerns that the city was becoming an even more dangerous place to live. One of the attorneys she worked with was mugged at the International Mall in broad daylight. "Fortunately the attacker was only interested in her purse, and she suffered only bruises from being knocked over."

Wyatt suggested that they all make a pack, "Nobody goes shopping alone. Let's go in groups of two or more, and preferably with one of us present," he indicated the three men.

The girls were in full agreement, and flattered that they were cared for so nicely.

"What about some mace for them to carry?" Chuck suggested.

"As I told Regina the day we all met, showing any kind of a weapon can provoke an assailant  to do more harm than they would unprovoked."

Frank passed the coleslaw, "There is a self defense class at Jackson where they teach people how to protect themselves and how to escape an attacker if they get a hold on you. We should all enroll in it."

"It's on Thursday evenings! Frances is going this week at Lamar's request. I'll call her and see if they have six more spots. Will that work with your call schedule, Wyatt?" Regina looked concerned for the safety of her friends.

"That will work out well, and we could all use a new adventure," Wyatt smiled.

Frances was delighted that they would all be coming. "I didn't know anyone in the class until now! The teacher is a black belt in Taekwondo and a very sweet person as well."

Vito Sicliano was as wide as he was tall, but could move with the speed and grace of a Cheetah. The seven friends thoroughly enjoyed meeting him and being in his class together. They learned basic and practical self defense maneuvers and gained a new confidence about their surroundings.

On the way home from work a few weeks later, Regina had her window open as the scorching sun beat down on the Volvo. Gas was too low to run the air conditioner and she didn't get paid until the next day. Stopped at a red light, she saw a car leave a parking lot to her right, even though the other light had just changed. The driver behind her laid on the horn ordering her to thwart the oncoming vehicle. Regina, remaining calm while the car cleared the intersection, was suddenly jolted by the tug on her hair.

Instantly she faced a large-framed Hispanic women with exceedingly big teeth growling at her as she shook her long auburn locks. Regina instinctively reached across with her right hand, grabbed the top of her attacker's head, closed her fingers tightly around the cropped greasy hair, and delivered a sharp right twist of her wrist, turning the lady backwards with her face now turned upward.

Delivering the self protective twist, she unintentionally yanked the woman's head into the car. Seeing the large angry face up closer, she rolled up window with her left hand, catching her intruder just below the nose and hearing her scream profanities as best she could in the awkward position. Securing her foot on the brake she blacked out but did not faint.

Two cars behind the "wrestlers," a police car had simultaneously emptied to get to the Volvo. Regina heard the loud voice saying, "Ma'am, you'll need to open the window. Open the window so she can get her head out."

In a moment that seemed like an hour, both officers standing by the car came into focus. One was restraining the trapped angry woman while the other was at the passenger door attempting to sell Regina on freeing the lady's head. Immediately lowering the window, she saw that the lady's upper lip was cut, and that her back appeared to be sore from the twist of her body during the counter attack.

Surprisingly enough the lady still had the ability to lunge for Regina again and to assault the officer who was still attempting to restrain her. With the aid of the other partner, the assailant was handcuffed and arrested. Since they were still blocking the flow of traffic, scanty information was collected. The first officer called Frank, and suggested that Regina drive home and allow them to continue interviewing her there, after the arrest was completed. Frank called both sets of parents and Chuck, who called Frances, who called Wyatt.

Frank was upset to say the least, and Chuck and Jeannie rushed downstairs carrying Dodger. Chuck embraced Regina informing Frank that Wyatt and Sylvia were on the way over with Frances. Regina could not understand the fuss, as she was unharmed and the lady was in custody. The Mc Brides were already in route and finally the Solbergs were coming, lest the fun could get out of hand!

Toward the end of the report, the four parents walked in, all of them more shaken than Regina. Dorothy started without greeting anyone, "Regina, what were you thinking! You really should" –

"Ma'am the officer interrupted, we need you to sit quietly or wait outside."

Dan flashed an understanding smile and stood against the dining room wall.

"We appreciate all of your concern, but we must ask you to allow Regina to answer, as she was the only one there," the annoyed officer continued.

After the report was taken, Raymond voiced his biggest fear, "Ah, Officer, will there be any charges filed against Regina? Our son is a medical student and we are concerned for his reputation." The remaining spectators were livid, but sensitive enough to restrain themselves. Except Frances – glaring at Dorothy and

Raymond she stated, "You two have the right to remain silent, so why don't you take advantage of it?"

The amused officer assured the group that Regina was the victim and had never left her vehicle. He explained the steps of prosecution and the fact that Regina would need to press charges. In true missionary fashion, Regina asked about the lady who had assaulted her hours earlier.

"She is being held and will be released on bond if her mother can scrape the money together. The family is afraid that Social Services will take her child if she remains in custody. The grandmother works as a waitress and cannot care for the little girl full time."

Regina asked if she would be allowed to see her attacker and the family, while Dorothy once again blurted out, "For God's sake Regina, you're not Mother Teresa. Just let the police do their job!"

"They were doing their job quite nicely when they asked you once to be quiet or leave," Frances snapped. Dan was covering his mouth with his hand to suppress his own laughter, and in an attempt to avoid another riot in Miami, while the others practiced their own forms of self restraint.

Answering the phone, Frances beamed and announced that Lamar was down stairs at the security gate. Twelve people would file into the Magistrate's office and then go to Shorty's for barbeque.

Regina was a beautiful picture of composure as she silently prayed, "Father if I let this lady go, will it make up for the litter box?" Laughing softly she added, "I should not joke around at a time like this. Please give me the courage and understanding to help this angry woman and let her see Your love and apply it to her own needs."

The lady was Graciella Bazarro, and her tiny mother, Bernadette Suarez, was wiping her own large frightened eyes. She spoke very broken English, which in addition to excluding Dorothy and her mouth from the conversation, prompted Regina to address her in Spanish.

The lady had emptied out her savings account of $300.00 and offered to give it to Regina and clean their house for one year for free if she would drop the charges. Regina smiled and embraced the little lady whispering softly that she had not filed any charges and would not. Adding that Bernadette must keep her money, she took a tissue from her own pocket to replace the worn out one, and dried the lady's tears. "We will clean our own house," she finished in English.

"When did she learn to speak Spanish?" Raymond asked nobody in particular.

"She always does at work," Frances answered.

"Regina had to know another language to work on the cruise lines," Dan added.

*"NO UNNECESSARY ROUGHNESS,"* Dorothy mocked in a singing voice.

Frank, who was too irritated to hold his temper any longer, demanded an apology, and got one.

Regarding the unnecessary roughness, to the dismay of both senior Solbergs, the reservation at Shorty's was increased by three. Dan, winking at Regina with admiration, escorted Grandma and the bruised Graciella carrying her little girl, Grace, who wound up in Regina's lap waiving a chicken leg and laughing, while her mother closed her own eyes in prayer.

Regina laughed as Frank teased her, "Way to turn down three hundred bucks, Polly!"

"Don't even try to pretend that you didn't enjoy little Grace just as much as I did!" Regina reached into her purse to retrieve her hairbrush, and finding a napkin wrapped around it, she immediately recognized her stepfathers script. *"No un-necessary roughness sounds good to me. In His name, please take this."* Three crisp hundred dollars bills accompanied the note.

# Chapter Eight
# When the Devil Needs a Snow Plow!

Unable to sleep, Dorothy Solberg sat by her orchids with a cup of hot tea. Her son had insulted her tonight in front of a room full of people and had allowed Frances to speak harshly to both of his parents. Regina was another matter, as they were fed up with her nonsense, and it was going to have to stop! The Solbergs were a close family before Miss goodie-two-shoes flitted in and took over. The kids needed to be taught a lesson, and she was just the teacher for the job!

Drafting her letter made her feel a little better, but she would not be content until it was mailed and answered.

Dear Frank,

You have insulted us tonight in your demand for an apology and by allowing your friend to publicly disrespect us. We regret the course of action that must now be taken.

UNLESS YOU AND REGINA PRESENT YOURSELVES
BEFORE US IN THE PRESENSE OF OUR ATTORNEY
WITHIN FIVE BUSINESS DAYS, AND SIGN A WRITTEN
APOLOGY AND A CONTRACT TO LIVE BY OUR RULES,
THE FOLLOWING WILL OCCUR WITHOUT EXCEPTION.

You and your wife will begin paying the mortgage on
the apartment at once, or you will move. Speaking
with our attorney, I understand that there is a way to
get both of your names off the deed. He will research
this tomorrow, in case this course of action becomes
necessary.

You will put the Volvo in your own name via the
enclosed title and pay your own insurance. All of your
school expenses are now your own responsibility and
you will reimburse us for the tuition and books that we
have already paid.

You will return your American Express card.

Regina will return the family diamond. Maybe God can
get her another one since she's such a hot shot.

In closing, "Mother Teresa" Solberg, is making a complete fool of you and of our family. Must cease!

Dorothy Solberg


The letter was sent Fed Ex the next morning.

Jackson Memorial was humming with the usual day's work and the team on the Hand Service was delighted with Frank and his performance. Extremely smart, he had a gentle bedside manner and his character was impeccable. Chairman Dr. Leo Gerehauzer, was a former Army Colonel with the appearance of still being in service. Well over six feet tall, had a straight and solid stance, and wore a crew cut. While he was the only attending who refused to wear a tie, his golf shirts were pressed, his white coat heavily starched, and his well-polished loafers could be used as mirrors. Feared by doctors, residents, interns, medical students, nurses, clerical staff and most patients, his voice could shatter the lights if he encountered the slightest deviation of his orders.

Leo Gerehauzer had noticed Frank's immaculate operating skills and was impressed by his self motivation and voluntary appearance on early morning rounds. Regina, having walked across to JMH at her husband's request carried a large basket of sandwiches and cookies so that the slammed hand team could grab a snack between surgeries. Entering the lounge she heard Dr. Gerehauzer mercilessly chewing the residents out, and stood quietly at attention until he had finished. The surgical team was shocked that she did not flee from the scene, and looked sympathetically toward Frank. Turning, the former colonel saw her and suppressing a smile asked in a loud voice, "What business do you have in the surgeons' lounge, young lady?"

"Dr. Gerehauzer, sir, I have brought all of you some lunch. With your permission I would like to deliver it."

Although it had been years since he was moved by such combination of sweetness and courage, since he had a captive audience, he continued to taunt her. "Do you have clearance to be here?"

"Sir! No Sir! Which is why I asked the Colonel's permission."

An amused smile spread across Dr. Gerehauzer's face as he took the basket.

"State your name, rank and serial number and who the lucky recipients of these contents are."

Smiling, but continuing her army voice, "Regina Solberg, Lollipop Lady at BPEI, no serial number, Sir! All of you are the recipients of the basket, Sir!"

"Am I to assume that I will partake as well?"

"That's what I said, Sir!"

Dr. Gerehauzer burst out laughing and motioned her ashen white husband forward to formally introduce him. Frank was proud of his wife and her ability to handle just about any situation gracefully. Her dedication to his profession was second to none, and it troubled him to think of the life she had given up for him.

"Leo Gerehauzer," extended his hand as a stunned room of surgical staff observed. "May I say that you put up a good fight, soldier? No offense intended."

"None taken. I hope you will honor me by having some lunch."

Regina had officially stolen his heart. Insisting that she join them for lunch, he devoured the turkey salad sandwich and some cookies, thanked Regina with a second very warm hand shake and ordered Frank to escort her back over to BPEI. Later in the afternoon, Dr. Gerehauzer complimented Frank on his skills and on his "lovely wife." Acknowledgement of a student by Dr. Gerehauzer was unheard of until today, and Frank was delighted.

Stopping at the security gate to sign for the letter he practically floated to the elevator, until he noticed the return address on the envelope. Regina was cooking to the beat of Latin dance music, while Monique tried to keep time with her tail. The apartment smelled like a French bakery.

Grabbing his wife he held her close and kissed her. Regina always appeared to be happy and carefree, but seeing the Fed Ex envelope, she inquired as to the origin.

"My parents. I'm not really surprised, but I have a feeling it's a threatening letter, designed to make us feel worthless."

"No one can make you feel inferior without your consent, Eleanor Roosevelt."

"Really?"

"Really hers, and really true! Open the letter, Frank, and let's see what it is before we assume the worst."

Frank was both scared and angry. Passing the letter to Regina, he put his head in his hands, "Are we really going to have to crawl to them?"

"When the devil needs a snowplow, darling."

"What do we do now? I should not have asked her to apologize."

"If memory serves, she was addressed four times by three different people, one of them a police officer."

"I am at a loss and I may have to withdraw from the hand service and work."

"Until school starts again and employment is prohibited. Great idea, but neither an option nor a solution." Regina was unimpressed by the threatening letter.

"What should we do?"

"We should answer the letter with a dignified counter proposal. If your parents will rent the apartment to us, we would be wise to stay here. If not we will need to move."

"The apartment is legally half ours."

"Not if your Indian giving parents want it back. Do you intend to go to court against them? Let's give it back and offer to rent it."

"The car! The insurance!"

"Elementary, my dear Solberg! The Volvo will be transferred to your name as requested. The insurance company will be changed to our choice, which they are probably not considering, as it will most likely rock their little umbrella."

"And your ring?"

"They can have the diamond back, honey, I usually only wear the engraved band anyway, and the engagement setting can be replaced with a synthetic stone when we can afford it."

"Absolutely not, Regina, they have no right to that stone. I think we should see an attorney."

"As you please, Dr. Solberg, but why fight when you can simply win?"

"Regina we can't get through medical school without them."

"We most certainly can! How does everyone else do it? Let's not look at it as getting by without them – but without their money. We do not have an American Express card, nor do we accept any living expense money aside from what will now be rent. There are loans available for tuition and books and we can handle the added living expense with one call."

"To who?"

"To the Arthur Murray Dance Studio. I can work evenings as

a coach and make more than we even need, while getting great exercise. Stop shaking your head no."

"We live in Miami, Regina, you can't be out in the evenings; it's too dangerous."

"Frank, the studio is well located to accommodate wealthy people who take very expensive lessons there. Sure, I'll need to be careful, but things will work out fine."

"I can't let you do it, honey, I'm sorry."

"We have no choice, and we should thank God that we have the options that we do," she said laughing, "while we ask Him to order my new diamond!"

"My mother has some nerve to insult God like that," an irritated Frank answered.

"More nerve than brains," the missionary nodded in agreement, "but so what, and what's with the attacks on Mother Teresa?"

"They're not that powerful, Regina, we could still fight this."

"They're certainly not more powerful than God, and we will fight it. With love!"

Regina went to the phone and called the dance studio. Because of her credentials, she was hired instantly with the ability to make her own hours.

Frank was trying to find a way to tell her that he needed to be there too, and she read his mind. "You can always join me and study in the back room. You can also be in my classes whenever you like and increase your already great dancing skills!"

"That will be O.K. with them?"

"Yes, Frank, that will be fine. They will pay me $50.00 an hour as a coach and $25.00 for classes."

Frank was amazed and nervous. What if Regina suddenly missed her dancing and decided to return to it? The money was certainly much better and the work far more glamorous. Setting the table, she glanced over at him, "No, Frank I am not returning to dancing as a career, we are simply at war. Why not have fun as we stomp the opposition?"

They had their dinner on the patio, discussing the hand service and the benefits it would bring to the future. Frank glanced down at the river, "What if we have to move?"

"Worse could happen, Frank. If we were forced to move it would end all financial ties to your parents and hopefully open a much more meaningful relationship with them down the line."

"Should we stay if they will rent the apartment? What if they decide to throw us out again with no notice?"

"There are laws that would keep them from doing that, and we wouldn't even have to fight them. They would be advised that we had so many days, during which we would look for somewhere else to live."

"None of this concerns you? We live in Miami, Pollyanna."

"We aren't the only people who live in a safe place in this big city. We can and will move if we are forced out of here, but for now, let's not borrow trouble. Your parents would be foolish to have this place empty while they look for tenants. They'd also have to travel back and forth or hire someone else to watch their investment. I think they'll let us pay rent."

The letter was drafted by Regina and faxed to the Solberg's to save time and money.

Dear Mom and Dad,

We are in receipt of your letter and are corresponding to the same via fax to accommodate your five day request. While we are truly sorry that you were offended, we will not appear before anyone and relinquish our independence.

You needn't research a way to get our names off the deed, as a mere request for us to sign them back over suffices. Please advise if we may pay the mortgage as monthly rent, so we can arrange to move in a time friendly fashion coordinated with the resumption of classes, if this is not an option.

The Volvo has been transferred, as you requested and we have assumed the insurance. The solitaire diamond will be removed professionally and returned to you via insured carrier. We have no American Express card.

Future tuition and bookstore invoices have been rerouted to us and your requested refund will be mailed within thirty days.

In closing, it is unclear whether or not you are fans of Mother Teresa, as you have mentioned her twice in less than twenty four hours. In case you are, we have attached the following copy of *"Do It Anyway,"* which hangs on this wonderful woman's wall, for your enjoyment.

Love,
Frank and Regina

# Do it Anyway

*"People are often unreasonable, irrational, and self-centered.*
*Forgive them anyway.*

*If you are kind, people may accuse you of selfish ulterior motives.*
*Be kind anyway.*

*If you are successful, you will win some unfaithful friends and some*
*genuine enemies. Succeed anyway.*

*If you are honest and sincere, people may deceive you.*
*Be honest and sincere anyway.*

*What you spend years creating, others could destroy overnight.*
*Create anyway.*

*If you find serenity and happiness, some may be jealous.*
*Be happy anyway.*

*The good you do today, will often be forgotten. Do good anyway.*

*Give the best you have, and it will never be enough.*
*Give your best anyway.*

*In the final analysis, it is between you and God.*
*It was never between you and them anyway."*

# Chapter Nine
# Rumpelstiltzkin - Cha-Cha-Cha

Dorothy and Raymond fully expected an immediate phone call requesting an appointment, and were thrown off course when the fax with a JMH cover sheet arrived instead. Snatching the letter from the machine and reading it, both were outraged. Dorothy headed for her kitchen, where she reached up toward the ceiling and effortlessly snapped the forty pound fishing line that supported the little Norwegian kitchen witch as it traveled back and forth across the room, prior to her tantrum. The imported decoration was a gift from Regina and the first thing in sight. She crushed the figure in her hands and dropped it into the trash can.

The next victim was the 11x14 picture of Frank and Regina on their wedding day that hung along side of the photo of Adam and Marge. As the picture was snatched off the dining room wall and smashed against the table, Raymond started crying like a child. "She has ruined our family. Never before has one of our sons treated us this way. He'll withdraw from medical school or she'll get him into terrible debt. Maybe her stepfather will pay his way through school. This will destroy our family name and Dan will once again move in like a big hero, the way he did at Shorty's the other night."

Dorothy, still fuming, sank into a chair, "They're ready to move out of the apartment that they could have owned in four years! That girl is such an imbecile."

Stanley Duncliff, the Solberg's attorney and friend of twenty-five years, knocked on the door and came in. Over lunch he tried to advise the Solbergs.

"The apartment is out of their names, and the diamond arrived by courier to my office this morning, complete with the certificate of authenticity. They asked for thirty days to repay the tuition which is very reasonable, especially since we have no grounds to make them to pay it at all. I don't think we could have forced their names off the deed either."

Dorothy, still in a rage, asked through her gritted teeth, "Where do we go from here?"

"I would let them rent the apartment for the cost of the mortgage and see what happens."

The phone rang and the state farm agent informed Raymond that Frank had changed insurance companies, striking the Volvo from the package that served as their umbrella.

Shuffling in anger he returned to his lunch. "Can we stop them from pulling out of State Farm? They have been our insurance company for years!"

"I'm afraid not, Ray, you really can't stop them from doing anything, given their ages and the legal system."

Dorothy poured cream into her coffee and motioned to a very peeved Raymond to pass the sugar. "We will rent the apartment to them for $100.00 per month plus the mortgage. I want them to be so stressed that the little princess goes back to her ocean- liners and returns our son to us."

"I can draw up a lease, Dorothy, but from the single time I've met your daughter-in-law, I can tell you that she doesn't seem the be the type to leave her husband for a better shake. What do you think, Ray?"

"I think they both love each other immensely but sometimes financial pressure can change that."

Stanley nodded pensively, taking a bite of his sandwich. He was impressed by the young couple's reaction to Dorothy's menacing letter, and he had a gut feeling that their plan to interrupt the marriage was going to go belly up. Quietly he hoped that it would."

Frank was up early and off to rounds as Regina prepared the crock pot for supper. Tonight they started at Arthur Murrays and both were excited about their new independence. Dr. Gerehauzer heard about Frank's schedule change and authorized it saying, "I'm glad he will be off evenings, days are the busiest for this service." The new lease, in Frank's name only, was faxed to JMH. After calling Regina about the extra hundred dollars a month, he signed it and faxed it back. Recalling her reaction as he pushed the start button, he was in once again in awe of her total state of calm. "It's still cheaper then moving, honey, and it makes them feel like they've prevailed."

"Have you told your parents what's going on?"

"Nope. It doesn't involve them and we want to keep the bad will to a minimum."

Frank smiled as he told her how much he loved her and returned to his work.

Arthur Murrays was a lavishly decorated facility by the Biscayne Bay. Frank was taken back when he saw the framed picture in the foyer displaying Regina Foglietta and her partner receiving the National Championship Award, and  witnessed the way Regina was received. Everyone knew her and seemed to feel privileged to sign up for coaching with her. The manager, Newton Daniel, was clearly at her beckon call, and welcomed Frank whole heartedly. Aware that having Regina in their studio would boost sales and enrich their staff performances, he told Frank to be sure she knew that the sky was the limit.

Watching the way she glided across the floor, Frank was reminded of liquid motion. Regina was beautiful, and it was apparent to any bystander that she was very much in touch with God. Well- known, highly respected, and admired by every person in the room, there was a humble, spiritual expression in her moves, and  Frank no longer harbored the jealous feelings he had until now, as he knew that she was dancing for his future.

Commanding attention by her mere professional demeanor, Regina conducted a fun but beneficial class for the staff. The

Latin dances were amazing and Frank intended to ask if he could join the next time. Newton walked by and jokingly asked Frank why he wasn't up there with the other victims. "I'm going to sign up with Mrs. Solberg tonight," he answered proudly.

"Mrs. Solberg, you have a student here who is waiting to sign up later. May he enter class now?" Newton indicated Frank.

"Of course he may!" Regina introduced her husband to the group, as each instructor welcomed him. Frank picked up the steps and their detailed technique with amazing speed and enjoyed the class as much, if not more, than everyone else.

Delighted when Regina chose him to demonstrate a Cha-Cha cross over, he felt both a new pride for his wife's true profession, and an added sadness that she had given it up for him.

Eating a delicious wine stew supper on the patio, he couldn't help noticing the glow in Regina's eyes, and taking her hand, he asked, "How could I have been so selfish as to allow you to give up your dancing for me?"

"You didn't allow it. Realizing how much I love you, I chose a new path to answer a calling of my own. I have no regrets, sweetheart. My dancing was always intended to pave the way for my missionary work, so it wasn't ever meant to be just glittery gowns and standing ovations. My art was for the Lord, and while I can still dance now, and I'll always have my coaching skills; as dancers age, flying splits and running lunges make their way to the younger champions. I always knew He had something else in mind for me, but I wasn't sure what."

Pushing back his chair to hold Monique, Frank asked, "How do I talk to Him as you do, Regina; how can I just get in touch?"

"His number is not unlisted, Frank. There are no secretaries to get passed and no appointments necessary. It's just that awesome, and the same love is available to everyone. Free gifts of this magnitude are often underestimated, and sadly bypassed, because they're misjudged as 'too good to be true!' "

Frank looked out over the river. He envied Regina's close contact with God that was as involuntary as her heart-beat. Noticing his expression, she continued,

"Frank, it's as easy as talking to me or to anyone of our friends. There is no fancy opening to recite, you just do it."

"How?"

"Like this," Regina selected her favorite star, "Jump in any time my Abba! I need some help here. Frank would like to know You as I do, and I don't blame him! Please guide this begging missionary of yours and stay with us."

"You talk to Him like that?!"

"Certainly. I wasn't disrespectful, as He knows my personality as well as He knows that every breath I take is His. I adore Him just that completely."

"So do I, but ....."

"Speaking of butts, your brother left a voice message for you to call him."

"Pollyanna! Did you hear that, God? Please forgive your tired little missionary, who just called Adam a butt. While I'm at it, please forgive me too, as I agree with her."

Frank was semi-stunned, but smiled in spite of himself.

"I meant that – the part where I addressed God."

"You're there then!"

Although Regina and Frank were tired from "burning the candle at both ends," they had more energy than ever. Each had a new bounce in their step and while nobody could identify the cause, the change had not gone unnoticed. The young Solbergs were having a ball and enjoying their new independence in the process.

Frank prayed to overcome the bitter feelings he initially had for his parents, and was slowly succeeding, as evidenced by his reaction to Adam's questioning.

Preparing to go apple-boarding on one of their long awaited breaks, the phone rang. Frank was surprised to hear from Adam at the early hour on a Saturday, and the pep in his voice during the response thoroughly amused his wife.

"Hi! How are you? And Marge, how's she?"

"There really isn't a problem, Adam. Mom and Dad are just as entitled to their views are we are to ours."

"Regina is my wife, Adam, and I will not allow any of you to disrespect her."

"Yes, but Regina isn't Marge; and we don't need their money."

"No, we really don't."

"So we'll rough it. Anyway, we are off to the beach! Talk to you later."

"Stuff, Adam, just stuff; but If you leave a message we'll answer the call when we can."

"No one is blocking any calls we're just not home that much."

Hanging up, the rebels burst out laughing as Regina grabbed the cooler and kissed Monique good-bye. Armed with their apple-boards, they were off to the shoreline!

As Adam reported the conversation, Dorothy and Raymond were wild with anger, while Marge was mentally decked out as a cheerleader, complete with huge pom-poms. Cleverly hiding her delight she placed her face in her hands for effect.

Dorothy looked at Raymond, "Where could they be every night? The phone just rings and rings! Frank is still volunteering on the hand service, so surely they're not out."

Raymond shook his head in disgust, "Did they send their rent?"

"Oh, yes. They sent their rent and a cheerful note, which I find antagonistic."

Marge noticed the absence of the second wedding picture, wishing it could be theirs. They were tied to the Solbergs to the point of insanity, and Adam would never dare to take a stand as Frank had.

Adam saw the hanging severed fishing line, but since he was enjoying his current status as number one son, he knew better than to ask questions.

Puffed up for the grandest with a newly acquired depth to his voice, he made a suggestion, "Why don't we call JMH and Bascom Palmer?"

His irritated parents answered in unison, "For what?"

"To find out what hours they're working, if they are working!"

"We have already tried to tap that resource, but The Privacy Acts prevent us from getting any information about any employee," the dismayed matriarch sighed.

"I didn't like the smell of this from the get-go," Adam boasted.

Raymond, deciding to finally include Marge in the conversation, addressed the still hidden face, "What do you think about all of this, Marge?"

Lowering her hands to reveal her eyes and nose, but keeping a firm grip on her mouth, she muttered, "Whatever."

Adam, disappointed in his wife's failure to cash in on a new position herself, tried to save the moment, "What about Regina's parents?"

"What about them?" Dorothy chewed on a piece of ice.

"How do they feel about this? Maybe they know something."

Raymond stood up and stretched, "If they know about it, they certainly won't be allies."

Opening the bedroom door, Raymond brought out a box of four kittens to be spayed, declawed, dewormed, flea treated, and inoculated, this afternoon; as the cheerleader in Marge's mind executed a series of deer jumps on her brother-in-law's behalf.

# Chapter Ten
# Crow is on the Menu

Dan popped open a can of beer and settled into his easy chair with the paper, while Elizabeth stayed engrossed in her murder mystery. Turning one of the pages, he looked over at his wife, "Have we heard from Pandemonium lately?"

"She called last week, as always. Why?"

"Because she's teaching at Arthur Murrays on Biscayne Bay, and it just seems odd that she never mentioned it."

"How do you know? I'm sure she would have shared that information."

"It's here in their advertisement," he read, *"Arthur Murray Dance Studio proudly presents former National Champion, Regina Foglietta, returning to the dance floor as Mrs. Frank Solberg, International Dance Coach and staff instructor. Exclusive instruction by appointment only."*

"Do you think they are having marital problems?"

"No, if that were the case, she would use her maiden name."

Picking up the phone, he dialed his partner. "Lamar? Hey, buddy, has Frances mentioned Regina leaving Bascom Palmer?"

"She was there today; Frances was talking to her while we were on the phone together. Why do you think she left?"

"She's working at Arthur Murrays on Biscayne Bay."

"I'll lay a bet that Frances doesn't know that, or she'd have told me. She's crazy about those two kids."

"Well, keep me posted, will you?"

"You bet, and do the same for me."

A knock at the door introduced Bub and Sis. They were the ones to be enlightened by *The Miami Herald* this time.

Bub lit a cigarette, "Why would Regina return to dancing, unless she just missed it?"

"Even if that were the case, why wouldn't she tell us?" Sis looked concerned.

Elizabeth, now worried, reached for the phone announcing her intent to call Arthur Murrays, as Dan quietly intervened, "Elizabeth, Regina is a very independent young woman. If we want information, we should get it from her, rather than calling her place of employment."

Walking into the room from a late class, Andrea caught the tail end of the conversation. "What's up, Mom?"

"Your sister is working at Arthur Murrays in Miami."

"She left the eye institute?"

"Not according to Lamar. He spoke with Frances today, and Regina was there."

Dorothy Solberg was at the end of her rope. She dialed the Miami Police Department and stated that she wanted to know where her son was night after night. Given her persistence, the confused Cuban officer on the line was as polite as he could be. After twenty minutes of badgering, he answered with frustration, "Look, Senora, you wahnt to know where he is, wet until he come home and ahsk him. We are nut bay bee seaters for adolts."

Slamming down the phone, she glanced over at Raymond, "They're so rude!"

Raymond, shoulder deep in his golf bag, was desperately trying to fish the fourth kitten out before it left a calling card. "Oh why don't we just leave a voice message and when Frank returns the call, let's just ask him where they have been!"

Following the usual three rings and the Florida Gator Fight song, she left her message:

"Frank, it's Mom. We have been trying to reach you kids and we were just concerned. Would you please call us?"


Bursting in from the dance studio, Frank grabbed Regina and Tangoed across the living room throwing her into a lunge. "Was that right, Mrs. Solberg?"

"That was right as rain, sir."

"Speaking of rain, we have a message."

Pulling the band from her hair and shaking it loose, she mocked, "Dr. Solberg how can you be so cold?"

Hearing the pleasant enough message he appealed to his wife. "What do we tell them?"

"The truth; we aren't bothering anyone, and we have done nothing that we have to hide."

The conversation was very quiet and almost awkward. Frank told his parents that Regina was teaching in the evenings to make ends meet and that he was with her for safety reasons and to take advantage of the free lessons.

His mother broke down in tears and explained that she had ripped down the kitchen witch and smashed their picture. Raymond was on the extension crying too. They both asked their son if they could visit. He explained that he would need to check both schedules and get back to them.

Regina was her usual understanding self, with her usual irreverent sense of humor. "So when does Rumpelstiltzkin and her blubbering side kick wish to grace us with their presence?"

"They want to come Saturday and take us out to dinner," he answered laughing.

"We have our exhibition Saturday afternoon, for the big promotion."

"After that?"

"Well, O.K."

"Are you sure, honey? Didn't you want to celebrate quietly? Just Us?"

"Your parents are hurting, Frank. Let them visit."

Frank returned the call feeling guilty that he looked forward to seeing his parents again. After all, they had been very cruel to Regina. It was he who prayed, "God I am concerned that she is suppressing the pain that has been unjustly inflicted upon her by my family. Please help us through this."

Regina was refilling Monique's pool while she whispered a

prayer of her own, *"Father, Big-Shorty and Short-Biggie are back in the picture. Please help me to receive them with grace and love, as I have neither to spare at the moment; but I am very tired. Thank you for this time away from them! I love you."*

Saturday afternoon, in front of an auditorium packed with spectators, Frank, in a black cut-away tuxedo, led his wife and dance partner onto the floor. Regina was radiant in a sea-foam colored sequin topped ball gown with her thick auburn curls cascading past her shoulders. The two made a breath-taking appearance, as the Master of Ceremony made the announcement: "Ladies and gentlemen, it is my pleasure to introduce the former United States Ballroom Champion and her new husband, Regina and Frank Solberg, dancing the Viennese Waltz."

Flying across the floor to the Blue Danube, they were spectacular. Frank and Regina were overwhelmed with love for each other and it showed. The crowd jumped to their feet and shouted for more. Firing off an impromptu Tango, they were equally fantastic.

Dorothy and Raymond were in the back row and four rows in front of them were Dan and Elizabeth McBride, Andrea, Frances McNeil and Lamar Mac Michaels, and Bub and Sis. While the two sets of guests were unbeknownst to each other, they were collectively attempting to surprise "the kids."

While the crowd continued their applause, Dorothy sobbed bitterly and Raymond was not far behind her. They had grossly underestimated Regina's skills and were shocked to see their son move across the dance floor like a champion, himself. Their well known and highly respected daughter-in-law had been working two jobs so that their son might benefit from the Hand Service! Thoroughly ashamed of themselves, they intended to slip back to West Palm Beach and call in their apologies. There was no way they could face their son tonight, much less his wife.

Andrea spotted the senior Solbergs and waved. The seven people in the McBride party moved toward them smiling, as Dorothy and Raymond froze.

Dan spoke first, "Did you guys know they were dancing?"

Raymond sniffling slightly responded, "Not until a few days ago."

"They don't know we're here," Elizabeth added.

"We were to meet them for dinner later," Dorothy wailed, "We heard they were dancing and got the last two tickets."

"What are you two bawling about?" Frances looked suspicious.

"Their beauty, their grace, and their love for each other," Dorothy dried her eyes.

"Oh! These are tears of joy, then," the sarcastic former army nurse continued.

Forced into parading to the receiving line, Dorothy and Raymond were shaken. What had these people been told? Regina's family seemed to know nothing, and Bub and Sis were also very sweet. Frances was probably just being Frances. If she knew anything she would have told Lamar, and he surely would have talked to Dan.

Arriving toward the front of the line, Regina was stunned and delighted to see her family. Her prayer was answered as she greeted her in-laws with grace and love. The exclusive fan club proceeded to the Melody Inn while the stars ran home to change. Regina grabbed the step stool from the closet and the scissors from the drawer. Reaching toward her own kitchen ceiling, she cut the fishing line that transported her own beloved witch from Norway, and kissing her good-bye, lowered her eyes, "I love you this much, my Abba." The little witch seemed sad as she was placed in her box for the trip to West Palm Beach.

Dinner was delightful and everyone joined in the conversation. Excluding the Solbergs, nobody had any knowledge of what had triggered the dance adventures. The Beef Wellington and all of the side dishes were extraordinary and the extravagant deserts were sinfully delicious. Dan alone noticed Regina as she slipped out of the restaurant to plant the small box in Dorothy's car. Whispering to himself he said, "Father our little Pandemonium has worked several different jobs, but when she works for You, she's the happiest!"

Dorothy was unable to sleep again, but for a much different reason. Raymond joined her on the patio, "We need to make this right, Dorothy."

Nodding in agreement she wiped her eyes. "She bought me another witch. Our Regina bought me another witch."

"Correction, she gave you her own."

"How do you know that?"

"Frank told me after you talked to him. He noticed the vacant line in the kitchen."

Touched beyond words, Dorothy could not converse anymore tonight.

Raymond called Frank the next day. "Where did Regina get the kitchen witches to begin with?"

"Cedars of Lebanon Hospital gift shop."

"Your mother is beside herself. She is very touched that Regina replaced her witch, but she also knows how much Regina loved hers."

"Perhaps it's time for the Solberg men to intervene. Let's buy another witch and replace Mom's. Then we can plan to get together and surprise Regina by hanging hers back up while she's at work."

"Frank, do you know where her engagement setting is? Mom and I want to reset the diamond."

"I know where it is."

"Would you please send to us?"

"I'll send it along with the witch by courier tomorrow."

"I'll hang Mom's witch in the morning, and we'll come down and hang Regina's   for her while she is at work; then we can all go eat at Kelley's."

"Sounds like a great plan; Regina is not scheduled at Arthur Murrays tomorrow."

Raymond hung the new witch while the jeweler reset Regina's ring. Was he imagining the happy expression on Regina's Norwegian import as he placed her back in the box to go home?

Upon being seated at Kelly's Seafood, the senior Solbergs begged Regina to give up her second job. The apartment was signed back over to all four Solbergs with no strings attached.

The waiter brought their appetizers and Regina was surprised to see a stuffed artichoke in front of her, as this item was not on the menu. Moving the fork, she saw a piece of glass. Frank took the ring from the plate and once again wiped it off, as his parents stood up and asked, "Regina, can you ever forgive us?"

It was Regina who was in tears now. The couples embraced and agreed that this type of error was never to happen again. As for the dancing, Frank and Regina decided to cut their hours back, but would remain involved for their own enjoyment and a little extra money. Four glasses raised and touched.

Unlocking the door to the apartment, Frank took Regina in his arms and hugged her before entering. The sleepy dancers embraced again, and carried  Monique to their bedroom. Regina went to the kitchen for a glass of water, and stopped suddenly, as she couldn't believe her eyes. The little witch rode her broom along the fishing line with a note attached to the handle: Dad bought me a new one, but it could never be as beautiful as your intent for me to have yours. This little witch needs to be in your kitchen, Regina, with all of our love.

The witch looked more radiant than ever, as if it were an angel saying, "He loves you this much!"

Tears streamed down her face, "Father, I don't know what to say. Thank you so much. I love you!" Retrieving the step stool again, Regina climbed up to kiss her beloved little kitchen witch good night.

# Chapter Eleven

# When the Scales of Justice Tip

Even though the temperatures didn't share the magic, fall was in the air. Typical excitement for the upcoming holidays lifted spirits everywhere. Almost everywhere. The Miami Court House rarely entertained gladness, as it was typically the stage of dreary, unpleasant circumstances. Sylvia had often shared the generic heartaches that she encountered daily as a court reporter, voicing her frustration with the legal system at large.

Enjoying their usual pool gathering, the six-pack was planning a big trip to the flea market next week. Frances and Lamar came over, bearing gifts for their three "grandchildren," Monique, Clementine, and Dodger, who were having a big time of their own upstairs on the Nugent's patio. The friends all noticed that Sylvia seemed downhearted, and made every effort to lift her spirits. While the men manned the grill, Frances and the other two women offered their help.

She had been assigned to a case that had the flavor of a vicious custody battle, for no other reason than money. The mother was a history teacher and had a three year child who adored her. The father of the child was a corporate attorney, who shortly after being retained by a model, found married life too restricting. Requesting the divorce, he offered equal property division and wanted no visitation. Recently, his new lady friend joined forces with his moral-free lawyer, making him aware of just how profitable a child could be when negotiating a settlement. The matter at hand was instantly transformed into a full blown ugly custody suit.

"I usually don't let cases get to me; maybe I'm losing my touch. The mother just wants a fair settlement and custody of the little girl. The father was very cooperative until his girlfriend and his lawyer realized how chunky the assets are. This is the most drastic turn of events that I've ever seen, and I'm having a difficult time separating my personal feelings from my work. This case makes me question how good I was at it to begin with," the burned out court reporter was close to crying.

Frances poured the lemonade while answering, "Sylvia, the fact that you recognize injustice and are upset by it, is hardly an indication that you're not appropriate for your profession."

Jeannie was sympathetic, "Attorneys in general make me sick. You know the old joke: 'What's the definition of a crying shame? A bus load of lawyers going over a cliff with an empty seat!'"

Their laughter brought the guys over to hear the joke. Wyatt was concerned about his wife as well. "She clutches Clementine like I'm going to fight for her, he teased. I've already hidden all of my socks!" He couldn't resist seeing Regina color once again.

Frances continued to laugh, and shaking her head asked, "Who's the father's lawyer, or can't you tell us?"

"It's public record, his lawyer is Steven Stokes."

Frances turned white at the sound of his name. Steven Stokes was an absolute pig with the morals of an alley cat. Mistakenly assuming that having a sloppy appearance helped him win, he was always disheveled and cocky with a vast rudeness thrown in for good measure. His callous face folded around his eyes and he reeked of laziness. Targeting easy money, he would stop at nothing and he prided himself in the heartless greed that he was notorious for. These traits all added up to Stokes being despised by most of the courthouse employee population.

Sauntering into Bascom Palmer one day to sit in on a patient's consult, the tall, heavy set, conceited attorney stood before Frances. Wearing an unbuttoned shirt, he revealed his very hairy chest, while clashing suspenders strained to support a wrinkled a pair of trousers. Announcing himself was his first and last mistake of the day. Clearing his throat, "I'm Steven Stokes, the attorney in town." Frances was unamused, "You don't say! Do you have an appointment?"

"I'm sitting in on the consult."

"Which consult might that be, Sonny? We don't allow unrelated people in the exam rooms."

"I'm a professional, lady," the insulted pig boomed.

"Not here. Here you're a nuisance, and a sloppy one at that, so don't bury yourself in the part, Perry Mason!"

The astounded lawyer stomped away, knowing when he was wasting precious time that could be used to gorge himself on a second breakfast. Waiting for the elevator, he soothed himself remembering that he could always say he was at Bascom Palmer, and lie his way through the rest of the evidence. The invoice would still be the same.

Frances popped a potato chip in her mouth, "Just remember, honey, right is right, and we should pray that this swine does not prevail."

"You know him?"

"I know him. Many have cowered to him, but don't you, Sylvia. God has placed you in this position for a reason, whether you know what it is or not."

Sylvia, after venting and getting grand support from her friends, looked better already. Wyatt was delighted, and addressed the ladies while confiscating the potato chips for the grill crew, "Hey, what did you guys do to her? You look better, honey." It was Jeannie who answered, "Regina gave her a sock and a bunch of change!"

Following hours of fun at the pool, the dim realization that the next day was Monday, concluded the cook out. Rounds of hugs and kisses circulated the group, encompassing the three canine "grandchildren." Grabbing a leftover chicken leg, Frank was curious about Sylvia's dilemma. "What was upsetting Sylvia, she's usually so perky?"

"An impending injustice, over money, that could affect a three year old child."

Frank quoted, "Money is the route of all evil."

Dropping Regina off to work, Frank walked over to JMH to grab the last of the opportunities on the Hand Service before classes resumed. Dr. Gerehauzer addressed him, "That was quite a photo of you and Regina in the paper, Solberg.

How long have you guys been dancing?"

"Regina has been dancing for years, but I just learned this summer."

"Impressive! Very impressive!" He continued with business as usual, "We have a little girl in the emergency room with a crush injury, and I wondered if you could work late tonight. I would like to have you scrub in with us."

"Absolutely, Sir, I'd be honored."

"Good then, and Solberg?"

"Yes Sir?"

"Hang on to that wife of yours. Most women would not be so lenient with your free time."

"To be sure, Sir."

As Frances and Regina expected, Bascom Palmer was also buzzing with business.

During a welcomed lull, Frances handed Regina a message from Sylvia.

"She was crying when she called, but I have no details. She asked in a whisper if we could meet her after work."

"Sure, in fact Frank is assisting in surgery tonight, and he'll be home late."

"Wyatt's on call too and Chuck is doing H&P's."

"Why don't the four girls meet at your house and have pizza sent in?"

"Sounds good to me."

Red eyed and shaking, Sylvia came to the door with Clementine under her arm.

The girls welcomed her while Clementine joined Monique and Dodger on the patio. Unable to talk, she burst into tears. Frances, remaining calm and speaking very softly asked, "What is it, honey?" Sylvia, trying to apologize for being upset, answered between sobs, "Steven Stokes wants a crucial slip of the tongue stricken from the record, but I can't do it. It is a key piece of discovery and he is livid that it's now on tape."

"Tough tomatoes," Regina was furious, "He can't do anything about it, can he?"

"He threatened me in the elevator," now in tears again, Sylvia continued, "He glared at me and said if I report him, he'll call me a liar."

"How did he threaten you," Jeannie shivered at the thought.

"He said that he will clear his desk and concentrate full force on bringing personal pain to me, if he doesn't have the corrected report on his desk in 24 hours."

Frances and Regina were more annoyed than scared, as Frances responded, "First of all, that mouthy pig is too fat and lazy to bring personal harm to anyone. He's vicious and that bears watching, but contrary to what many believe, he's not above the law, and he knows it."

"He sounds like a bully to me," Regina's New York savvy was surfacing.

"Do you think he would hurt you?" Jeannie was petrified.

"I'm afraid that he would stop at nothing," bursting into a new set of tears, Sylvia snubbed, "He lives at the Doral."

"Regina's eyes lit up," Do you know where?"

"Three buildings over from us; months ago, I saw him getting out of his car."

Frances answered the door and set the piping hot pizzas on the table. "We need a plan," she said, handing out plates, "Sylvia, you must not go anywhere alone, under any circumstances. We need to notify the police department, whether that fat jackass calls you a liar or not."

"The bigger they are, the harder they fall. Let's stand up to him, let him know that you're not afraid of his threats, and that the police are involved," Regina was on her feet. "We will pray for guidance, but this thug can't go around threatening people; I don't care who he is!"

Sylvia was weak from crying, "I wonder if he can find out where I live? I wish we weren't on the first floor."

"What does Wyatt think about all of this?" Jeannie wondered.

"He thinks we should report it."

"Good," Frances went to the phone. "They can take the report from here."

Two officers were at the door in minutes. They took the report and advised Sylvia, and then left to pay Steve Stokes a visit.

Flicking the porch light on, he answered the door, annoyed to see the police officers. Listening to the allegations, the confident lawyer grinned and shook his head. "She has some kind of a crush on me, and propositioned me in the elevator. I didn't think anything of it, so I just let it go." The officers advised Stokes that everything so far was hear-say. The one taking the report, did not believe that Sylvia propositioned anyone, and spoke in a no nonsense tone,

"Since you are a lawyer, I'm sure that I needn't remind you that communicating threats is against the law."

Sporting a cocky smirk, the lawyer responded, "So is making a proposition and filing slanderous complaints. If the lady wants court action, I'll give her all she can handle." Closing the door, he returned to his den and offered a smug toast to the once beautiful buck that hung mounted over his gas log fireplace.

Three days later, Wyatt came rushing down to the clinic. "Regina, can I borrow your car, mine is in the shop, and Sylvia needs me at home?!"

"Of course," Regina tossed him the keys asking, "Do you need help?"

Frances, walking briskly towards them said, "Regina, go with him, I'll cover."

Sylvia was hysterical. She had dressed for work and walked into the living room to bring Clementine in from the patio, when she saw his huge angry face, grinning at her from the glass door. He pointed at Clementine in his arms and seeing Sylvia faint, he left the scene. The police were on the way, as Regina called on her own sources, "Father, please help us. Please don't let this man hurt that little dog. Give us the wisdom to safely assist our friends and soften this man's heart with Your love." Steven Stokes was not at home when they drove by his apartment, and there was no barking or visible sign of Clementine.

The usual, no proof, no witnesses, no action, scenario left all of them heartbroken. Regina packed Sylvia's overnight bag and took her to Isla Del Mar. Wyatt was on call tonight and she would clearly be unsafe there.

Jeannie and Frances both got relief and came over at once. Regina had already decided that this was going to stop. She called Steven Stokes from a pay phone while Frances kept watch. "Mr. Stokes, I am a student in need of money. Do you need a witness? I could've seen or heard anything, if you know what I mean."

"What's your name?"

"Justine, I never give my last name up front, if you know what I mean."

"What are you looking to make, Justine?"

"I need one thousand dollars for school, if you know what I mean."

"What are you willing to do for it?"

"Well, I don't want to hurt anyone, if you know what I mean."

"Suppose you come over tonight and we'll have some drinks?"

"I work at night as a waitress. Can you meet me this afternoon?"

"I suppose I can."

"Fine, where do you live?"

The address matched, but where had he put Clementine?

Frances, Jeannie and Sylvia stayed back in Jeannie's car while Regina, disguised in a dark wig and glasses, went to the door.

She shivered when she saw him, as Steven Stokes looked like he was capable of anything. There was no sign of Clementine, but Regina thought that she might be in the apartment. Frances and Jeannie moved towards the door while Sylvia stayed close behind them. "May I use your restroom?" "Justine," asked.

"Second door on the left; what do your drink?"

"What do you have?"

"Beer, liquor, soda, … …"

"Beer! I love beer."

Going to the restroom, Regina quietly pulled back the shower curtain. Horrified, saw Clementine crammed into a small carrier appearing to be dead. Regina flushed the toilet and turned on the water. She reached into the kennel realizing that Clementine had been heavily sedated, but was still breathing.

Walking back into the living room, she said, "I need to get my purse from my car, if you know what I mean." Opening the door, she motioned the others in, while Stokes was in the kitchen getting the beers.  Frances noticed the desk chair with wheels. Motioning Regina to distract him, "Justine" went into the kitchen and put her arms around his neck. "Well he snickered, we can earn money in more ways than one." Frances rushed the chair forward against the back of his legs, as Regina helped to thrust the large man into it. The others wasted no time. France secured his fat legs together with duck tape, and fastened them to the bottom of his chair, while Regina shoved her wig in his mouth. Sylvia and Jeannie held his arms while the taping process continued. Regina ran back into the bathroom and brought the kennel out. Easing a listless Clementine out of the wet and dirty box, she handed her to Sylvia. Sylvia wept as she took her little dog in her arms. "Keep her warm," Frances spoke over her shoulder, and let's get him away from the windows," she coached, as she Regina and Jeannie wheeled the heavy chair into the den. Sylvia noticed an imported throw on one of the living room chairs, and wrapped her little dog in it, as the gagged lawyer tried to wiggle in protest on his way down the hall.

Although the angry face was terrifying, the four ladies were not shaken.

Regina did not speak, but returned to the kitchen where she had spotted the tool box. Opening the lid revealed a small electric circular saw. She returned to the chair as the others watched in shock. Frances was speechless and the other two were stunned to paralysis.

"You seem to like to inflict terror on others, Stokes," Regina smiled.

The gagging lawyer was petrified. Plugging in the saw and starting it Regina walked toward him as he squeezed his squinty eyes shut. Changing course, as she had planned, Regina moved toward the sickening trophy above the mantel and standing on an embroidered chair, removed the antlers while the fat lawyer struggled to free himself. Turning off the saw and calmly returning to his chair, Regina and Frances were planning their departure. Looking Steven Stokes straight in the eye, the former army nurse spoke in her military voice, "If you report us, we'll just call you a liar."

Regina was next to enjoy a face to face encounter, "If you so much as walk by any of us, we will haul you before a judge, and

Buster, we have four witnesses. Oh, and I'd advise you never to hurt another animal again. If you get board, try bathing."

Stokes was now attempting in vain to scream, as Jeannie and Sylvia eagerly started out to the car to rush Clementine to the vet. Regina yanked the wig out of his mouth and Frances took the empty soiled kennel and forced it over his fat head making sure that he could breathe through the vents. After cutting one of his hands free, they slowly walked toward the door ignoring his frantic, screaming threats. It would be awhile before he could free his head from the stench filled kennel, not to mention his fat legs and feet. They burst out laughing and hugged each other, "Which one of us gets to take the heat from Abba?" Frances asked, still laughing. " We'll share the blame, if there is one. I'm sure He isn't thrilled about the way His children were treated, not to mention Clementine and Bambi."

The flea market trip was cancelled to move Wyatt and Sylvia to the third floor of their building. Steven Stokes withdrew from the custody case enticing the father to settle. The mother settled for full custody, generous child support, and half of the estate, and the court reporter gained a whole new confidence knowing that the missionary gangsters were overseeing things, and that they were protected by the most powerful Warrior of all!

# Chapter Twelve
# To See or Not to Sea

Vibrating sounds of the helicopter landing on the roof interrupted the cheerful hum of conversation in the Bascom Palmer cafeteria. Emergency announcements blasted over the intercom, *"All triage staff to the clinic. All triage staff to the clinic."*

Frank and Chuck had stopped by for lunch at Pollyanna's and were as stunned as the crowd they encountered, while they witnessed the emergency air transports arriving at the institute. Critically wounded patients flooded in from over occupied hospitals near Port Everglades. Seconds passed before their pagers went off calling them to JMH, stat.

The news reporters were swarming the medical complex, as the television announced the tragedy: "A tidal wave hit the MS Sonofjord ocean liner at 4:00 am injuring hundreds of passengers and crewmen. Miraculously, there were no fatalities, as the ocean-liner was expertly maneuvered through the 30 foot wall of water, by Captain Victor Brentzen, of Norway, who has been on the seas since age thirteen. According to port authorities, turning the ship so the wave washed over her, enabled her to topple over and come back to the surface, resuming her upright position. It was an act of genius, resulting in the deck chairs being the only losses to the sea! Injured passengers have been transported by air to the local hospitals while the over flow are being taken to Jackson Memorial Hospital, and the Bascom Palmer Eye Institute in Miami."

While Fort Lauderdale got the bulk of the injured, JMH and Bascom Palmer  were also packed, keeping transport on their toes, and staff at work around the clock. Frank was called to Orthopedics, second year student or not, to help the hand team. Within twenty four hours, everyone was stabilized, and the JMH complex received national recognition for the excellent performance rendered by all of the services within it.

Frank and Chuck were exhausted, but still not cleared to leave the hospital. Wyatt joined them in the cafeteria the next morning for breakfast. Frank had seen the news, and was beside himself. He broke down, as he told his closest friends about Captain Brentzen. Wyatt reassured him that the captain had a blow-out fracture and would be released in a few days. "Regina has been nowhere near him, Frank."

"If Regina is meant to return to the sea, what right do I have to stop her?"

Chuck buttered his toast as he answered, "Well, for starters you're her husband.  Frank, Regina is a one man woman; she's not going anywhere."

"I watched her dance and teach professionals to dance. She's beautiful! She gave all of it up for me because I asked her to."

"Because she wanted to," Wyatt corrected, "and in case you haven't noticed, my friend, she has a mind of her own!"

"And a very stable one," Chuck added.

"And a sock," Wyatt laughed as the others followed suit, unable to help themselves.

"Should I go to see him?" Frank asked in desperation.

"For what?" the two spoke in unison.

"I'd rather know what I'm dealing with; what she's dealing with."

Chuck shook his head, "Brother of mine, nobody's dealing with anything. Regina is a very religious lady dedicated to God. She may not flaunt it or ram it down everyone's throat, but that's part of how she wins so many over and puts them in touch with Him."

Wyatt nodded, "He's right, Frank, Regina is married to you, not to Captain Brentzen. She's staying right here."

"Does Frances know about him?" Chuck asked.

Frank shrugged, "I don't know whether Regina has mentioned it or not."

"We could page her over here; confidentially, I mean."

"I don't know, Chuck," Wyatt, shook his head, "What if Regina doesn't want anyone to know about him?"

Frank nodded in agreement, "She is very stern about her personal space, and definitely no blabber mouth, as we saw when my parents pulled their nonsense. She never let on or told anyone about it. Her own family didn't even know, and probably still doesn't."

"That's the code she lives by. I see it all the time at work and so does Frances," Wyatt added.

"I'm going by the clinic to see her before I go home and crash." Frank mumbled, looking terrible.

"Call if you need us," Chuck stood to leave.

"I'll keep you posted, Frank, he's right on my floor. He probably doesn't even know Regina works there. It's very unlikely that they will just bump into each other," Wyatt reassured.

Between signing people in, Regina was fixing sandwiches when he arrived. She looked worried, as she walked over and kissed him. "Can you go home and sleep? I left your lunch in the fridge with a note."

Frances took one look at Frank and knew he was troubled. Wanting to help, she waited until Regina showed the next patient to an exam room, and reminded Frank about her license to meddle. "I'm worried about the captain from the cruise ship. He's upstairs with a blow-out fracture."

"According to the news he's going to be fine. Is he a friend of yours?"

"No, he was in love with Regina."

"Well that was then and this is now, Frank."

"Has she mentioned him?" Frank asked, fighting back tears.

"Not once."

"I need her to see him. She needs to see him, Frances."

"Then take her, Frank."

Kissing Frances goodbye, he left for home, hoping to sleep.

Regina came in with her arms full of packaged fresh Spanish mackerel. "One of the patients was giving bags of these away. Frances and Wyatt got some and I got some for us and for Chuck and Jeannie!"

Frank took the bags from her, asking if she wanted him to cook them fresh for supper and save the spaghetti sauce for tomorrow. "Whatever you like; are you too tired to grill them?"

"No, and it would be a sin to freeze them, when we can eat them fresh. Why don't we call Chuck and Jeannie and see if they want theirs now as well?"

"Great, I have some news to tell Jeannie anyway!"

"What news?" Frank looked hurt.

"They are selling giant bags of beads at the flea market, and we're going to make jewelry out of them. Sylvia knows how and she will teach the rest of us."

"Oh," Frank responded, feeling two feet tall.


The girls threw together impromptu side dishes of parsley noodles, salad and crescent rolls, while they chatted with excitement about the upcoming bead mill. Jeannie motioned to Regina that something was up. "Frank, we're going up to Jeannie's to get some extra tea bags, we'll be right back."

Jeannie told Regina about Frank's concerns and how upset and worried he was.

Regina looked solemn, "I know, Frances told me after he left to come home. How can I reassure him? I didn't know he was aware that Victor was at Bascom Palmer."

"It was on the news; he saw it in the surgeons' lounge."

"Great. The man lives across the world and winds up at my place of employment!"

"Have you seen him?"

"Oh, no! No, I don't think that would be wise at all."

"Well you didn't hear it from me, but Frank wants you to see him."

After the grill was cleaned and the dishes were put away Frank came into the kitchen. "Do you want to see him, Regina?"

"Not particularly."

"I think you need to. I really think you need to see him, if only as a friend."

"He's not my friend, or yours either."

"Why don't we go see him together?"

"Are you trying to get rid of me?"

"No Pollyanna, I'm just trying to be sure you're really mine."

"How could you possibly not be sure?" Regina answered quietly, but in a voice he had come to recognize as the one she used when she meant business.

Victor Brentzen was a handsome man with typical Norwegian features. His blonde hair and deep blue eyes, matched the fair complexion. Tall and very well built, he made a striking appearance, especially in his uniform. He was recovering nicely from his injury and enjoying the attention from the press.

Charmed by his accent and flirtatious personality, nurses were in and out of his room far more often than was necessary.

Frank's heart pounded as they stepped off the elevator. Walking into his room, Regina gave him a friendly hug and introduced Frank, who extended his hand.

Victor was obviously taken back when he saw Regina, and he

felt that she was still his. Gathering all of the information he could, he planned to see her alone as soon as the opportunity presented itself. He was an international hero now, and after all, it hadn't been that long.

Following the brief visit, the Solbergs bid the captain farewell, and walked toward the elevator. Frank studied his wife, looking for any signs of interest, but found none. He would be glad when the captain returned to the sea and prayed that he'd return alone. "God, please don't let him take Regina! Please help me through this resentment that I have for this man, and help him to recover, and leave. Soon."

"He looks good, don't you think, Polly," Frank tried to sound nonchalant.

"He looks normal, but his injury was not all that serious."

"Don't make me beg, Regina, what do you think of him?"

Looking steadily into her husband's eyes, Regina spoke sternly. "I think that Victor Brentzen is a self impressed, pompous, player. The recent flattering news hype is not likely to humble a man like that. Victor loves attention and you saw how the nurses are carrying on over him. Three came in to check on him in our short visit, taking un-necessary blood pressures and fluffing his pillows in the presence of visitors. Can you imagine what goes on when he is in the room alone, if he ever is.? Patients in the ICU don't get that kind of attention. Now if you'll excuse me, we have real patients to care for here."

"What if he wants us to have dinner with him?" Frank called after her.

"Then you let me know how your steak was when you come home."

Frances gave Frank a thumbs up as he walked back over to JMH, feeling a little better.

Victor was disappointed to learn that Frank Solberg was not on call as a second year medical student, and as far as anyone knew he did not work at night. He was also annoyed that he was right across the street and frequented the clinic for lunch with his wife. Victor had missed his chance with Regina. Sitting idle in the room, he recalled the way Regina looked on his ship. Always smiling, always bubbly, <u>always straying from scheduled tours to seek out the poor people in different countries and help them in any way she could</u>! The latter had always annoyed him. Victor was continually troubled by her independence, and her closeness to God, in Whom he did not believe. She didn't flirt or try to look sexy, but had a warmth; a natural beauty, that men like Victor found threatening.

He wondered if he would feel differently now, being an overnight hero. Picturing Regina shaking hands as his wife, he tried to imagine the fuss that awaited him back in Norway. Maybe having a woman who stood out as Regina did was the answer after all. He let his mind relax as the parade of nurses returned.

During early rounds, Dr. Wyatt Clements checked the captain noting his excellent progress on the chart. Victor inquired about Regina, as Wyatt played dumb. "There is a red headed lady named Regina Solberg who works here. Can you get a message to her? She is an old friend of mine."

"I'm sure that I can."

"Please take this letter to her in the strictest confidence. Oh and Doctor, take her the flowers in that blue vase. The nurse who brought them is off for the next two days."

Wyatt, was not accustomed to being a porter, but wanted to keep a close eye on his friends, so he agreed."

Regina and Frances were planning the jewelry lessons when he stepped off the elevator with the flowers and the letter. Passing the arrangement to Regina he relayed the message, including the origin of the flowers, and complaining that he wasn't even offered a tip!

Regina set the flowers behind the counter as a patient handed her half the sandwich she had made for him to exchange it for a peanut butter and jelly.

Obliging the young patient, she returned to the desk and asked Wyatt if he was returning to the floor. "Yes I am, will there be a reply, Madame?"

Taking a dollar from her pocket, Regina handed him the plate holding the  returned half sandwich, answering, "Why yes young man, please give this to Captain Brentzen; and note that we Americans' tip," she added, handing him the dollar.

Frances burst out laughing and was hoping to read the note, if she was invited.

Opening the hospital envelope, they read:

> Regina, we have made a terrible mistake. I still love
> you and I can see in your eyes that you still have
> feelings for me. Return to the sea with me, the best

captain in the world. I am leaving for Norway tomorrow, but I can send for you.

Please see me in my room, as I think it best to meet
here.

Love to you, always,
Captain Victor Brentzen

"Nice. Note the way he signs, 'Captain?' The world is one big mir-
ror to him."

Frances was delighted. Proud of her 'adopted' daughter, as
usual, she was touched that she was included as she read the note.
Indicating the blue vase of flowers, Regina asked, "Do you know
of a home for those? If the nurse who gave them to him ever got
wind of this, she would be hurt by it. From the looks of that arrangement, it cost a small fortune."

"If it wouldn't be awkward for anyone, I wouldn't mind having it. Those can be planted from cuttings."

"Be my guest."

The first opportunity she got, Frances went over to JMH to exercise her license to meddle. She knew that Frank was worried
and she was bursting with happiness for him. After relaying the
events of the morning, which had already been partially reported
by Wyatt, she was delighted to see the grin spread across Frank's
face, followed by an expression of pure relief.

Seeking even further reinforcement, Frank walked into the
bedroom as Regina was brushing her hair. He loved to see her

hair softly falling about her small shoulders. "Wyatt said that all of the nurses think your captain is dashing."

"Yeah, he sure is. I wonder if they realize that he's dashing around with more than one of them?"

"How do you know that, Mrs. Solberg?"

"Because I know him, Dr. Solberg."

"I'm not even a doctor yet," some of the concern returned to Frank's voice.

"But you will be one day, and you are something now that the captain about whom you fret will never be."

"Yours?"

"A gentleman. And mine."

Frank took his small wife in his arms and held her tightly, hoping she wouldn't see the tears trickle down his cheeks. He spoke from his heart, "Thanks so much, Father. Thanks ever so much!"

The next morning the captain stepped off the elevator in full uniform. He was, dashing. Frances thought he was one of the best looking men she had ever seen, and was a little worried that he showed up. In a charming Norwegian accent he asked to see Regina.

Going into an exam room and leaving the door open, Regina sat down in one of the two visitors' chair while Victor chose the second. He looked at her dark brown eyes and flaming auburn hair. She really was the top of the line, and he wasn't sure how she had gotten away from him.

"You got my flowers and letter?"

"You got my sandwich?"

Amused as always by her quick wit; he laughed softly. "Will you see me in Norway, Regina?"

"Not unless a tidal wave blows Miami in your direction."

"I can make a beautiful life for you, Regina."

"I love my husband, Victor, and we have a beautiful life."

"You make too much of a deal about the customs of men who live on the sea."

"You make too little of fidelity."

"What does that mean, Regina, I am not familiar with all of the English words."

"You are certainly not familiar with that one, but if you look it up in the dictionary the definition will say, 'Not you, Captain.' "

His silence was the result of a new realization, a new feeling for Regina. She was a very fine woman, but too much woman for a sea captain. This exotic lady must belong to some god somewhere. Maybe her God was real.

Checking his watch, he stood and smiled at her. "I'll always love you, Regina."

"You do that, Victor." Offering her hand, he shook it.

Frances was conveniently outside the door polishing the glass that housed the fire extinguisher, while exhausting her license to meddle.

Victor left the clinic and got into the waiting limousine with a distinguished middle aged blonde lady who was to accompany him back to Norway.

# Chapter Thirteen
# Happy Half Doc

Platters of rolled cold cuts and deviled eggs lined the counter, while bowls of potato salad, macaroni salad, and coleslaw, were on stand-by in the refrigerator. Crock pots simmered with baked beans, Jack Daniel wings, Jamaican meatballs, and cocktail franks, as Frances, Regina, Jeannie and Sylvia scurried about happily preparing the rest the feast.

Frank and Chuck had officially completed half of their long haul through medical school, and reception room bordering the pool at Isla Del Mar had been reserved for the big bash. The guest list included the six pack, each couple's parents and in-laws, Frances and Lamar, Andrea , Uncle Bub, and Aunt Sis.

Frank was particularly nervous because Dr. Leo Gerehauzer wangled an invitation a few days ago, as a result of a joking hint to Regina, and he wondered what impression the chairman would walk away with.

Once Dorothy learned that the Gerehauzers were attending the party, she insisted on having it catered. Regina politely informed her that this was not only the Solbergs' celebration, but everyone else's as well. Persisting as usual, Dorothy had called three more times to educate Regina on protocol and to stress the importance of the family name with the Gerehauzers.

Desperately appealing to Elizabeth, Dorothy was told that since she and Dan were not asked to bring anything, they weren't. "Well I think they are going to make fools of themselves if we don't intervene. Cold cuts and salads are insulting to people like the Gerehauzers, who now obviously view Frank as an equal."

"It's my understanding that Dr. Gerehauzer received the invitation from Regina," Elizabeth responded coolly.

Calling Regina one last time, Dorothy ranted on, "I'm pulling rank Regina, do you want paella or bouillabaisse for the party?"

Trying to remain calm, Regina again explained, "Mom, neither of those would be appropriate as this is a pool party, and all of us have already coordinated the menu. If you would like to bring something, we can certainly use veggies and some of your wonderful dip."

"Don't patronize me, Regina," Dorothy barked, "you have Frank call me as soon as he walks in."

Frank returned the call and was short and to the point. The party was not hers to host, and she was to be a guest. Period.

The six-pack had been up late last night decorating the room that were now filling with food. Jeannie had planned the desert table, which was set to emphasize a large marble sheet cake reading *Happy Half Doc*, placed among assorted Italian cookies, miniature cheesecakes, brownies, Jordan almonds, M&Ms and small bowls of salted mixed nuts.

Cold cuts, cheeses, rolls, salads, deviled eggs, relish trays, and condiments set on iced bases filled the next long display, while hot items were stationed along the wall so the crock pots could be plugged in.

Introductions were made as the guests arrived, and everyone helped themselves to cold drinks and finger foods. Dr. Gerehauzer introduced his wife, Hazel, a tall attractive blonde with blue eyes, who instantly fit in with the other ladies. Jeannie's parents, Bert and Ann Sawyer, were a delight as well, while Chuck's were likened to the senior Solbergs! Sylvia's mother, Hyacinth, was visiting from Jamaica, and added a fabulous flair to the group, while her father, Roger, a quiet man, joined Dan, Bub and Lamar. Regina introduced Dr. Gerehauzer to her stepfather, as the former colonel extended his hand, "Leo Gerehauzer, do you know that I love your daughter?" The "distinguished guest" blended right in with older men, while everyone else mingled happily.

Well after the party started, Raymond appeared at the doorway with a mammoth pan of bouillabaisse, as Dorothy followed with a network of hot plates.

Interrupting the celebration, unabashed, she insisted, "This needs to be plugged in," while moving the entire hot table to accommodate the pungent fish stew that she was firmly told not to bring.

Frank was livid, and ready for action, when Regina intervened silently, "Father, please help us to handle this situation with understanding and compassion."

"Sweetheart, I forgot that Mom was bringing a hot dish, can you help me relocate two of these crock pots to the other side?" Both Leo and Hazel Gerehauzer knew what was going on and each gave Regina an understanding smile. Frances walked over to assist, relocating the items on the buffet. Dorothy, who could never leave well enough alone, spotted the Gerehauzers and started in a nice loud voice, "Oh, hi Frances, I'm rescuing my daughter-in-law's party. I can't believe she was going to serve finger foods to such elegant guests." Laughing she continued, "When I heard what was on the menu, I thought I was going to die!" "Sounds good to me," Frances snapped as Leo Gerehauzer muffled a laugh. After disrupting the entire display, Dorothy and Raymond introduced themselves to the curious guests.

Jeannie immediately matched up the two sets of in-laws, "Rob and Connie Nugent, meet Dorothy and Raymond Solberg; you four should get along!" Giving Chuck's parents a gentle shove of dismissal, she moved to the other side of the room. Dan and Regina dared not to look at each other as they knew they would burst out laughing, while Bub, Sis, and Elizabeth were all in the same boat.

The party continued as the guests talked and laughed comfortably.

Dorothy once again had to ascertain that she had saved the day and in a louder tone than before, put her two cents in again, "Regina! Where are the dishes? Surely you don't intend to serve bouillabaisse on paper!"

Frances walked over to Regina, and making absolutely

no attempt to lower voice asked, "Honey, is your apartment locked? I'll go help Golliath haul the glass dishes down here." As they turned the corner the entire room burst out laughing. Leo Gerehauzer pointed toward Raymond who was joining in the fun and warned, "Buddy we got you over a barrel, she's bigger than you."

Hyacinth, added sweetly, "Whoa Dahlin, she bigger den everybudee!"

Dan was laughing so hard he couldn't talk and Regina was right there with him. The guests all loved Regina and they didn't appreciate Dorothy's digs.

As dinner was served, Dorothy approached Leo Gerhauzer and said, "You know, Frank is interested in an orthopedic residency, but I understand the field is very competitive. Is there anything he should be doing to get his foot in the door?"

Elizabeth mumbled softly to herself, "Yeah, he should put his foot in your mouth!" Hazel turned slightly to hide her laughter, and motion that she agreed whole heartedly.

The Colonel popped open the cold soda in his hand and answered matter-of-factly, "He should hang on the Regina. We're hoping to steal her for our department, and Frances too."

Dorothy forced a smile, "Yes, we're very proud of her ourselves," she gushed.

"I'll bet!" Hazel mumbled to Elizabeth.

Frank had relaxed and realized that people are people and the Gerehauzers were just as human as everyone else. The jokes continued, but all in good fun and out of Dorothy's earshot. Wyatt accidentally broke a plate and Frank was telling him not to worry about it. Chuck put his hand on Frank's shoulder, "You're a big man, Frank. Not as big as your mother…" as everyone, including Frank and Raymond laughed.

Water volleyball began and continued until the players were too exhausted to go on. Cake and ice cream were served as Hazel, mocking Dorothy, quietly said,

"Regina, where are the dishes! Surely you don't intend to serve baked Alaska on paper!"

Thoroughly enjoying the party, the guests stayed on until evening, when both old and new friends embraced each other. Regina's family, and Frances and Lamar stayed to help clean up. Dishes and silverware, which were not part of the plan, were even more unappreciated now, than originally! Andrea shook her head, "She is such a control freak! How do you stand it, Regina?"

Uncle Bub, walking into the kitchen for a cup of ice, added, "We were all very proud of the way you handled her, honey, and Frank is raving about you. He intended to make them take that garbage right back to their car."

Regina smiled, "Frank's mother is always a challenge, and after today, I see that Raymond also gets fed up with her."

"Who wouldn't," the usually passive Aunt Sis spoke up, "She's ridiculous."

Dan came in from the patio with Monique in his arms, "You must be referring to Golliath," he continued to laugh heartily.

Frances munched on a handful of nuts, "That stew was disgusting! Dorothy needs to be enlightened to the fact that she's not running a brownie troop."

Pollyanna, living up to her nickname and her mission, giggled, "Look at it this way, if she hadn't made that big scene, we wouldn't have half the laughs that we did!"

"Isn't Hyacinth adorable?!" Frances recalled the little Jamaican lady's contribution.

Following the clean up the family left to go home, and the laughing young Solbergs hugged each other. Frank looked admiringly at his wife. "What pray tell, are we to do with the leftover gruel that my parents shoved down everybody's throat?"

Regina answered laughing quietly, "Well, Frances insisted that they take it home for Marge and Adam, since we didn't want to deal with it."

Frank threw his head back laughing, "The Gerehauzers had a ball!"

"They're lovely people, Frank, and both spoke very highly of you."

"On their way out, Dr. Gerehauzer shook my hand and said, "Regina gives a whole new meaning to the phrase 'hostess with the mostest!'"

"I think everybody had a lot of fun; the party was definitely a success."

"Yeah, well I could've killed my parents for pulling that little stunt!"

"I didn't appreciate it either, but it all turned out well, and nobody got hurt."

While Regina disposed of an overlooked plate of cake and ice cream, Frank walked out to the patio. "Can I call you Abba, too? I noticed that Regina calls you, my Abba, which I recently realized wasn't the name after all. Abba is Father, and my Abba is Pollyanna's subtle way of letting You know just whose Abba You are! I told her she has to share! Thanks so much for seeing us through, Lord, and please help me to understand my parents. Give me the wisdom to withhold information that could be a trigger!"

The next morning Frank was off to the hand service, supplied with a carload of party leftovers. Regina and Frances had a very slow clinic, as most of the doctors were at a seminar, so they went to JMH for lunch.

The indigent clinic was a disaster! Similar to BPEI before Pollyanna organized it, the noise and confusion were unbearable. Dr. Gerehauzer had already heard about the BPEI clinics, and consistent with his military background, he wanted the same for JMH. Taking the opportunity at hand, he sat down with the two girls and made himself a sandwich from leftovers. Leo was never known for his tact, and today was no exception, "How can we steal you too from BPEI, *Basic Prima Donna Elite Inn?*" Bascom has more money and donations rolling into it than they need, and we're in the red!"

Frances, among her own, returned fire, "Orthopedics is one of the most lucrative fields in medicine; so if you guys are in the red, I would explore billing and collections. As far as the clinic goes, this chaos is ridiculous. Pollyanna and I could have this place up and running smoothly, if we were given the clout to come in and do it."

Looking at Regina, he answered, "Well, Pollyanna, what say you to that?!"

"Frances and I work well together, and I can see that this clinic does need work, but we would have to cover Bascom Palmer before we could even think about transferring."

"Fine, so you two go find coverage and train whoever you need to. I'll get with JMH administration and promote the paperwork."

Frances was thoughtful, "Can we brainstorm the offer and let you know, Colonel Sir?" she asked smiling.

"Sure, I didn't expect an answer now. Tomorrow will be fine. Understood?!"

"Sir, yes Sir," both girls answered at once.

"Of course we'll need a raise," Frances added.

"My salary is fine, Regina corrected."

"No, young lady, your salary is not fine," the colonel stood up to return to the clinic. "Do you want to starve or resort to eating that crap your in-laws hauled to the party? You are in demand! Frances, I'll let you negotiate the salaries."

Walking back to BPEI Frances spoke first, "Would you be interested in transferring? You do realize that BPEI will fight to keep us, including matching any offer JMH makes?"

"My reason for the transfer would be to make life easier for the patients, as we did where we are."

"Then you would move?"

"Maybe, would you want to leave?"

"I'm ready for a change, and as Leo says, we are a prima donna facility."

"Could we leave all of our supplies here for the new people?" Regina was already having second thoughts.

"JMH will provide whatever we need, and Lamar and your father have a meeting here in the city tomorrow. We'll see them for dinner, and see if they can assist if any remodeling would be necessary."

"I'll talk to Frank tonight and see what his feelings are. We wouldn't be working together, and once summer ends he'll be a third year and won't be on the service at all."

"That's not a problem either way, JMH is huge and many relatives work there."

"Frances, I understand that the clerical help over there harbor a great deal of racial prejudice. There are twenty four women in patient services alone. We would most likely be crossing paths with them."

"We'll cross that bridge when we come to it. Leo Gerehauzer won't tolerate any nonsense, and if we're being brought into the department to straighten it out, we'll have his full support.

Returning to their posts, Frances saw the message: Nurse McNeal, please call Dennis De Sanko at JMH. Dennis De Sanko, Administrator for Orthopedics, was an easy going middle aged man who loved fun. He ran the department loosely and allowed everyone to kind of, "do their own thing." Frances would never allow a setting like that and Regina was also very organized. If this transfer ever did materialize, all parties concerned were in for a big change.

# Chapter Fourteen
# Orthopedic Transplants

While Frances and Regina paused to blink, the summer had come and gone. They were training their replacements while simultaneously visiting JMH. Offering to increase their salaries, and provide full reign, Dennis De Sanko looked forward to an outpatient clinic like the operation at BPEI, and had discovered in the interviewing process, that Regina could cut to the chase in collections! Dr. Gerehauzer had asked Dennis to plant Regina in billing and Frances in the clinic, so they could discover the roots of the problems.

The main problem in finances was that the insurance companies were not being billed accurately, and Medicare forms were hardly being processed at all. Instead, employees in Patient Services were coming to work late, after stopping by the cafeteria for full hot breakfast trays to go, and eating them at their desks while talking until after ten in the morning. Lunch hours were even more abused, and Regina was surprised to see that Dennis walked in and out, oblivious to the conduct, and how it was viewed by outsiders. She and Janet were the only "white" girls in the office, and Janet had already shared the secret of "playing along or being abused."

Regina called all of the insurance companies, Medicare, and Medicaid, for the purpose of establishing a contact person in each office. Having done that, she filed late forms and followed through by communicating directly with the people with whom she had previously spoken. Thanking her new contacts each time for their assistance, made communications pleasant and cost productive. Within forty-five days, money was rolling in like waves. "Collecting is nothing more than sales," she explained to a delighted administration. Many years prior, having been trained in sales as a new dance instructor, it was said that Regina could 'sell Henry Ford a Chevrolet.'

Frances and Regina met with administration with a list of suggestions, which were implemented as policy the following day. The Board of Directors met and voted to have Regina head the billing and collections operation, which did not entice her in the least. "I am not a paperwork employee, so if this is the new deal, I'm not interested." Dennis was annoyed with her reaction as her salary was well increased to compensate her for the transfer. Displaying management characteristics for the first time since he had come to Orthopedics seven years prior, he flexed his muscles. "Regina, Dr. Gerehauzer is no one to mess around with, and this is where he wants you."

"I'm no one to mess around with either, and I am respectfully refusing this position; it's not what we agreed to."

"You tell that to Dr. Gerehauzer," he shouted.

"No, you tell him," Regina answered quietly, "I am returning to Bascom Palmer."

Frances looked up from the desk, and went to Regina immediately.

"What happened, honey, you look upset?"

"*'Dennis, Let's have a ball De Sanko,'* informed me that I am to work full time in collections, so my end of the deal is off!"

"Does Leo know this?"

"Not yet."

"Well when he finds out he'll set it right, or we'll both withdraw our offers."


Regina loved working with people, and the fact that the department of Patient Services had been permitted to turn into a three ring circus was not her problem. Frank was worried that Dr. Gerehauzer would be angry with her, and reveal his wrath to the small framed redhead. His panic skyrocketed when he played the messages and found that Regina was expected at a mandatory administrative meeting at 8:00 o'clock the next morning.

"Look, honey, the department is in shambles, and they need you. If you just announce a change of heart, you'll be fine."

"I don't give a rat's backside if the department is in shambles or not. That's Dennis's little red wagon; and I don't have a change of heart."

"You're not afraid of Dr. Gerehauzer?"

Regina smiled, "I'll go with God, and He's a lot higher than Dr.

Gerehauzer. We were promised detailed positions with Orthopedics, and I will accept nothing that deviates from our agreement."

Frances was on the phone, "Did you get the message about the meeting tomorrow?"

"Yes, are you going to go too?"

"Yes, but I love the way they just assume that we can be there, since we are still at BPEI."

Dennis De Sanko was a relatively good looking man and was very popular among his staff. He always flashed a big smile and often used inappropriate language to appear more hip than his position called for. Flirtatiously he approached Regina offering her coffee and saying, "Look, Dr. Gerehauzer is just trying to give me what I need to straighten this place out," Regina.

"Really? Well he should start by gifting you with a spine, and a cerebral cortex wouldn't hurt either."

Leo Gerehauzer had just stepped out of the elevator and overheard the conversation. He rushed into his office closing the door behind him, so that nobody would see or hear him laugh. Dennis had made the mistake of assuming that dealing with "Pollyanna," was going to be a piece of cake. Wait until he tried crossing Frances!

The meeting began right on time, and Leo Gerehauzer called Regina to the front of the room. Bending slightly to look her straight in the eye, he articulated clearly. "Mrs. Solberg, this department needs you and Ms. McNeal. It has been brought to my attention that you are unhappy with the assignment that has been given to you."

"That is correct, Sir."

Putting his arm around her shoulder he turned her to face the long table of big shots. "Now, Mrs. Solberg, in a nice clear voice, I would like for you to tell us exactly what you want, while we record it and put it in effect immediately."

Addressing the group in a loud voice he continued, "Understood?"

Winking at Frances, he left the room.

Without Regina overseeing billing and collections, the money quickly stopped coming in. The clinic was running like a charm, though, and the indigent patients were delighted. The head of Pediatric Orthopedics, Dr. George Easterlin, was overjoyed. Children were kept happy and consequently quiet, while their parents were delighted with Pollyanna's treats. Residents and orthopedic technicians swarmed in for snacks, and to do efficient cast applications and removals without being hunted down as before. Frances and Regina worked beautifully together, and were well liked by everyone in Patient Services.

Dr. Easterlin, was a former army friend of Leo's and also a retired colonel, but he was far more easy going than his colleague. In his early sixties, he had six adult children of his own and several grandchildren. Seeing the progress that had been made, he was impressed to say the least. Both he and Leo Gerehauzer stopped by for lunch, and to "make an appointment" to see Regina and Frances. The girls looked at each other and laughed. "We can see you now," Frances suggested, as Pollyanna served them their lunch. The two attending sat quietly at first, then Leo spoke. "We have a big problem. The money has stopped coming in, and we wondered if we could combine your jobs with overseeing the processing of payments and the efficiency of the staff across the hall at Patient Services.

"Now we would, of course, leave your offices right here. You two would just lay down the law and keep the money coming in." George Easterlin continued,

"We have been told that we can have this whole side," sweeping his arm to clarify the possible new space, "and a full set up to make the indigent children and their parents more comfortable, if the money starts rolling in again. We can also provide funding for the parents to stay with their small children while they are in the hospital recovering from surgery." Leo carried the ball again, "When pediatrics is not in clinic, the hand service would be, so the space would be well utilized. I want to stress that Pollyanna would remain with the patients."

Frances answered, "Considering the condition that patient services is in, there would have to be drastic and immediate changes."

"Name them," Leo reached in his pocket to withdraw a pen and small notepad."

The army nurse was re-enlisted :

1.  "Breakfast is to be eaten before coming to work, No food at the desks.

2.  A time clock is to be installed.

3.  Lunch time is one hour, period.

4.  No personal phone calls or visitors on hospital time.

5.  Work will be delegated in a manner in which it can be tracked.

6.  All insurance/Medicare/Medicaid forms are to be filled out the day of the visit or the next day at the latest.

7.  Doctors will write the diagnosis on the chart legibly, so the billing clerks can read it.

8.  Administration will develop a check and balance system that Regina can easily reconcile and have efficient knowledge of anyone who is falling behind in their responsibilities; so that the bulk of her time is spent caring for the patients."

"Will that be all?" Leo asked, smiling, "Regina, do you have anything to add?"

"No, Sir, I think Frances covered everything."

Walking to their cars, the ladies were laughing. "Leo knew that this place needed a good shake up, and that's why he brought us over. He's an excellent surgeon, but he's also a very smart business man."

"Dennis is going to buck the time clock," Regina smiled, "he doesn't believe in them."

"Fine – then there's no deal."

The next morning Dennis approached Frances about her demands and let her know that if she insisted on the changes, there would be a walk out in patient services. "Don't warn me Sonny, warn the cafeteria. Anyone who walks out is opening a job for somebody who will start off properly."

Dennis knew better than to pursue the matter, and made his way to pose as the hero for the upcoming oppressed across the hall.

The staff was furious and treated Frances with cold indifference, and Regina with blatant rudeness. Dropping by for the patient rosters, Regina was told that nobody knew where they were. Indicating a short stocky lady with an attitude the size of Texas, she asked, "Gwen, I believe it was in your job description to generate the rosters, was it not?"

Gwen got right up in Regina's face and answered, "Look, honkey, I may be black, but I'm no slave!"

"Nobody asked you to pick cotton, Gwen, so cut the racial nonsense. This has nothing to do with being black, white or chartreuse. Consider yourself warned that if the roster is not produced in fifteen minutes, the incident will be reported."

While Gwen was laughing at the warning, Regina couldn't help but notice a what a lovely smile she had. Turning to leave, Gwen followed her. Regina continued toward the door, while Gwen, annoyed that she did not seem intimidated, continued to shoot off her mouth, "You and Msssss. Frances are prejudice, and that can get your butts fired."

"I can't speak for Frances, but I can tell you that I am prejudice," all mouths dropped open in shock.

"You admit that your prejudice, white girl?" Gwen squinted.

"You better believe it, and actually I'm more of a tan color."

"You just said that you are prejudice, in front of all these witnesses."

"That's right, I did, and I am. I am prejudice against people who are lazy, narrow minded, and who don't give a rip about anything but their paychecks."

Now walking toward her steadily, Regina caused Gwen to back up, "and while you're taking note of what I say in front of witnesses, you are far too attractive to pose as a gangster, so give it up, sister."

Gwen and the others were dumbfounded as Regina calmly left Patient Services.

Just under fifteen minutes later, Gwen walked in and handed Frances the rosters, glaring at Regina. Regina opened the jar of chocolate kisses on her desk and offered it to Gwen, "Candy?"

"Yeah, I'll eat your candy, white girl." Gwen grabbed a huge handful of the candy and started laughing, as she opened the door.

"Tan, I'm tan," Regina answered, and opening the door after her, added, "You're welcome."

Frances looked up and smiled at her. The girls in Patient Services were going to have to shape up or ship out, and they knew it. Clinic was running smoothly when Frank and Chuck came in for lunch. Dr. Easterlin was in the market for a sandwich himself, and greeted Frank warmly. "Fella, these two girls are fantastic, and Orthopedics is fortunate to have them."

"Thank you, Sir, I agree." The three men in white coats watched Regina as she circulated among the little patients.

Pediatrics had a miraculous effect on Regina, as she loved children.

A little girl with a spine disorder called out, "Geeena, I'm not going to X er ray!" Regina Picked the little rebel up and whispered, "Cassandra, why don't you want to go to X-ray?"

"Because someone will get the Big Bird doll, and I won't see him again like last time."

Regina smiled as she carried the child to the chair where Big Bird waited, and took both to X-ray. "When you come out, you can take Big Bird home with you." The child put her arms around her neck and kissed her.

The next day Regina entered her office as Gwen was leaving with all of her candy. "It's gone white girl, I got every last bit of it."

Throwing up her hands, Regina responded, "Tan, tan, I told you I'm tan! You didn't get all of the candy, by the way; in fact, the jar was almost empty. Taking a bag of chocolate kisses from her drawer, she handed them to Gwen. Now you have all of the candy. AND I'M TAN!"

Gwen did not know how to react, but when she tried to glare at Regina, she couldn't help laughing. "Alright, Ms. Solberg, you tan."

Over the next few weeks Regina chipped away the wall between the clinic staff and Patient Services. Dennis De Sanko was very impressed and had come to enjoy walking through the outpatient departments. Money was pouring into the department along with high morale. Regina asked Frances if they could appeal to administration for the employees in Patient Services to receive monthly bonuses based on their collections. "It would give them the incentive to go the extra mile. They would be more willing to work side by side with insurance companies and Medicare, if the result was an extra check for them."

Frances liked the idea and had it approved within a week.

The staff across the hall was thrilled. Maybe the white girls weren't so bad after all! They asked Regina to help them form good rapports with insurance companies, and followed her lead. The training sessions were fun, and as Regina did mock collection calls with the girls, they were able to learn how to work the system to their advantage. The staff dressed more appropriately, and conducted themselves more professionally, as they were taking a new pride in their positions. Frank enjoyed his visits to the clinic where someone always complemented him on his wife.

One of the chief residents came into the clinic and noting Frank's picture on Regina's desk, asked, "Oh, are you his wife?"

Regina looked up and answered without smiling, "He has a wife?!"

"Very funny," Frank popped his head in the door a couple of hours later. "Pollyanna, don't you know how important our family name is," he mocked.

The Solbergs were happy working together and the department was happy to have them.

# Chapter Fifteen
# Prison Fights

Clinic schedules were packed, but the work was rewarding and Regina had never been happier. She was with her husband whom she loved immensely, and with friends who were as close as any family might be.

During the afternoon rush, the clinic door burst open and two armed guards shoved a prisoner into the waiting room. The man had fallen from scaffolding while doing community service, and appeared to be in a substantial amount of pain. Shackled and humiliated he was taunted by the guards. Regina was furious! She immediately showed them to a room and offered the man some lemonade. The guard spoke up, "No ma'am, he can't have refreshment; he's not here for a party."

"Nobody said that he was," she answered, "and I wasn't talking to you," she defiantly handed the prisoner a cup of lemonade.

The guards exchanged glances, but did not interfere. Offering each of them a drink and a sandwich, she also served the prisoner.

Regina proceeded to take the history and again corrected

the guard for answering. She was kind and gentle to the patient which irritated the escorts.

"Who is your supervisor?" the first guard demanded, wiping his mouth on his napkin.

"I'll get her for you," Regina answered pleasantly.

Frances entered the room and listened to the complaint while Regina stood quietly.

"The prisoners who are brought here are in our custody, and not to be entertained," the guard bellowed.

Frances remained very calm but very stern, "The prisoners you escort are both you prisoners and our patients. Once they enter this clinic, they will be treated with the same dignity as any other patient. They are paying their debt to society on your turf."

The prisoner devoured his sandwich and Regina handed him another one. Finally, after giving him a box of the bubblegum band-aids, the guards were outraged.

When the patient was brought to X-ray, Regina learned to her horror, that some of their residents also treated prisoners cruelly. They made it a habit to insult these patients and would often set their joints without anesthesia.

As the doctor read the X-Ray that revealed a dislocated shoulder, the patient looked up at her. He was sedated for the relocation, but clung to Regina's hand for dear life. The shackles were placed on his ankles for the trip back to the prison, as his arm was in a sling. Regina called for a wheelchair and positioned a blanket over the patient's legs to conceal the heavy shackles. The guard gritted his teeth and said, "We are not wheeling this prisoner out; he can walk."

"I am wheeling the <u>patient</u> out," Regina persisted, "then he will be your prisoner."

"I'll have your job, lady," the gruff guard shouted.

"Suit yourself," Regina smiled tossing him a bag of suckers, "give these out to everyone we pass on the way to the car."

The prisoner didn't dare to laugh, but he wanted to. He could have kissed Regina.

The next morning Dr.Gerehauzer came into the clinic for a cup of Regina's cappuccino with bit of orange candy in it for extra flavor. Taking a seat on the edge of her desk, he asked Frances to come in. Steaming cup of coffee in hand, he got right to the point, "Soldiers, what's eating Warden Gordon?"

"Hopefully something slow and painful, if he's affiliated with the prisoner who was seen here yesterday," Frances responded coolly.

Gordon Robertson, the prison warden, was a bitter man with hardened features that masked his good looks. He was tall and thick framed with wavy salt and pepper hair and grayish-blue eyes.

"Regina, a guard is threatening to file assault charges against you for throwing a bag of suckers at him."

"Good, I like television," Regina smiled.

"Television? How does television play into this?" Dr. Gerehauzer was amused as usual.

"I think the citizens of Miami would be fascinated to know that prisoners are being manhandled, especially after the tragedy with Arthur McDuffie just cleared the air. Gordon Warden should thank his lucky little stars that this report will involve a white man."

Ever so slightly shaken, the colonel answered, "Regina, honey, we don't want to involve the media, do we?"

"We're not the ones wetting our pants because someone, after being asked to, tossed a bag of suckers in our direction."

"He asked you to?"

"He said he'd have my job."

Leo Gerehauzer and Frances both laughed, as Regina calmly stirred her coffee.

Looking up through dark solemn eyes, the troubled clinic coordinator continued, "Dr. Gerehauzer, I have been told by the X-ray technicians that some of our residents take it upon themselves to set prisoners' joints without anesthesia."

"Who was your direct source of this information, honey?"

"Nancy Lopez, the supervisor. I accompanied the patient because I saw that he was petrified. While he was in X-ray she told me, and added that someday we are going to be called on the carpet for it, if it ever gets in the earshot of the wrong person."

Dr. Gerehauzer looked concerned and angry. Reaching across her desk he picked the phone and called his office. "Sharon, I need to schedule an emergency meeting of all Orhtopedic staff, including residents."

Warning both the ladies in his company, Leo spoke quietly, "You two be prepared in case Robertson saunters by for a meeting, as he has advised Sharon he would do. Should he come here, say no more than 'good morning,' and page me. Understood?" The two ladies answered respectfully, "Yes, Sir."

Risk Management was called and the hospital attorney,

Melinda Thompson, responded quickly. "Mindy," barely five feet tall, was a very bright, and very sweet lady. She located the prisoner's records and met with Dr. Gerehauzer. "Leo, your girls are correct; this man's rights have been violated, and I'm glad the staff stood up for him. He is serving time for embezzlement, and doesn't have any record of ever hurting anyone."

"The crux of the problem is that he <u>does</u> have a box of bubblegum band-aids,"

Leo laughed, as he pictured Regina over-ruling the burley guards.

"Solberg sounds familiar," Mindy drummed her pencil. There was a medical student named Solberg here when my mother came in for appendicitis."

"Frank Solberg is a third year medical student and a prime candidate for a residency in the department here. He is Regina's husband."

"Well, I doubt that they'll file an assault charge, but if they do, between stone wall McNeal and the lollipop assailant, the prison will be the laughing stock of Miami!"

Leo thanked Mindy for her rapid response and walked her to the door.

"I know Frances, so I'm not a bit concerned there, but is Mrs. Solberg upset; do I need to reassure her?"

"Pollyanna never gets upset, she was delighted with the possibility that the guards would be exposed as a result of their own stupidity."

"I'll be in my office if you need me, Leo. If the warden does schedule a meeting, I should probably sit in on it."

"You'll be the first one I call."

George Easterlin walked in the clinic door, hugged Frances, and started laughing. He was walking to his office last night and saw the prison guards grumbling like two old ladies while they struggled with the wheelchair. Attempting to show off, the first guard put his foot between the prisoner's two feet to yank him up from the chair, and caught his own foot in the shackles he forgot were there. He lost his balance and fell back against another car, with the prisoner leaning on top of him. "That poor old guy looked like somebody snatched his Sunday shorts," he called over his shoulder, still laughing. "Good, it's about time those macho men were put in their places," Frances answered the colonel in motion.

Frank and Chuck came in for lunch with Wyatt. Regina and Frances hugged him, inquiring how things were going at BPEI. "They really miss you guys over there."

"Frances and Pollyanna are opening a clinic at the prison!" Chuck laughed.

Frank enlightened Wyatt, as the three guys ate sandwiches and cookies; and then stepped into the waiting area to do a quick puppet show, as the children bounced with excitement. Regina watched with pride, as he was wonderful with the kids in clinic and with his patients. When she told him about the prisoner, he was as annoyed as she was.

The conflict with prisoners being seen in the clinic continued while various guards were awakened to the changes in personnel there. Warden Robertson was getting irritated with the reports, and made a mental note to contact Leo the next time there was an incident of disrespect toward one of his escorts. It wasn't long before "Warden Gordon" would revisit his entry, as Regina had no intention of yielding on her standard of care for all patients.

Late one afternoon, as the clinic was closing, two guards escorted a prisoner who had accidentally crushed his fingers in a closing cell door. Having been detained in a traffic jam with a malfunctioning air conditioner, they were already in bad humor. The small, older man, stood sweating in shackles, while the guards flipped open ice cold sodas from the vending machine. Regina handed him a cold cup of lemonade, as the escorts rolled their eyes. "Ma'am, we don't allow prisoners to take refreshment of any kind whatsoever," the one guard announced rudely.

"Well then it's a good thing that it's not a call you get to make." Regina was tired of this game.

"We have to be somewhere at 7:00 sharp, lady, and we don't have time to fool around with you."

Handing the prisoner an ice pack for his hand and a sandwich, she replied, "The emergency room is open, Sir, while we technically are not. You will "fool around" there for hours if you don't like our service. Just let me know which way you want it before I page the doctor back here."

"You are interfering with the law, lady, and you can be prosecuted for it. This man has a debt to pay to society for a crime he committed."

"We are not a collection agency, nor do we fall under your prison rules."

Frances came back from across the hall as the second guard

spoke up, "Warden Robertson himself is going to file a complaint against you people and you'll be fired."

"Good, we have more work than we want. Sit down, Sonny, I'll make the threats around here," Frances was not in the mood for after hour prison nonsense either.

Leo Gerehauzer came in surrounded by residents and took care of the delighted patient. Following his treatment Regina handed him a box of bubblegum band-aid's, as the angry guards clenched their teeth. The girls noticed that neither of the tough guys attempted to converse with Dr. Gerehauzer. They saved their big show for women and people who were conveniently in shackles.

Regina sat out on the patio looking over the river, while Monique selected different toys to shake and discard. She was not able to take her mind off the prisoners who had visited the clinic. Bowing her head she whispered, "Father, is there some way I could work with those people? I see a deep sadness that doesn't seem to relate to the crimes they may have committed. Can we bring some hope to these prisoners and the staff that work among them?"

Frank came in from the hospital and sat with her. "Why so glum, chum?"

"I'm just thinking about the prisoners."

"What about them?"

Regina's eyes filled with tears, "There must be something we can do to give them hope."

"Pollyanna, life can't be made of cotton candy. People in prison are there for a reason."

"Agreed, I'm not implying that they aren't, or that they should not serve time. They just don't necessarily deserve to be handed a life sentence, caused by relentless emotional damage while they're in custody. Frank I've seen quite a few prisoners come into the clinic being treated like scum of the earth. We don't even know why they are in prison, but we know it can't be too serious, or they would be in a high security facility."

"What would you suggest then?"

"I would like to promote something that they could benefit from when they've completed their sentences. They could walk away with something beside bitterness and resentment. "

Frank was very preoccupied with his wife's missionary drive to help anyone she thought could be in trouble. He was no fan of the incarcerated and did not share her compassion for them. Mentioning his concerns to Chuck, he was relieved to have his support. "I would definitely not allow her to have anything to do with inmates, brother, it's just too dangerous."

Wyatt had a similar reaction, "That sounds like Regina, all right, but I would find something else to take her mind off it."

Another encounter with the prison gave Regina a new insight. One of the two guards accompanying a very large male inmate was threatening to "hurl" the lemonade and snacks if she took one more step. Regina answered politely, "You are responsible for your conduct, Sir, and if it is out of line, security will be called."

The guard grabbed Regina and slammed her into the wall, as patients screamed.

Frances leapt to her feet and backed the guard against the opposite wall with a chair at his throat. The prisoner dropped to the ground face down and covered his head. Security rushed into the clinic and escorted the restrained guard out while one of their own men replaced him. Regina was upset, but unharmed.

Frances set the chair down, and everyone, including the prisoner, stood and applauded, as she hugged Regina. Risk management was the next on the scene.

The staff acted quickly to move the patients into rooms and out of the way of any media that could possibly show up. Frances and Regina quickly composed themselves and moved on with their work. Leo Gerehauzer came through the back door as the news reporters came through the front. Reacting to a microphone shoved in her face, Regina smiled and addressed the uninvited visitors, "We were practicing for our church play and I certainly hope we didn't cause any alarm." No stranger to cameras, she then mimicked a loud whisper, "As much as we would like to visit, as you can see there are patients here, so we'll have to excuse ourselves and return to work."

Pointing the microphone to Frances, the reporter asked her what just happened. "Are you deaf? You heard the girl, we were practicing for a church play with the hospital's permission, which is more that you have to be here. We are compelled to return to clinic now; the way you came in is the way to leave."

Disenchanted, the reporters left in search of some bystanders who might have a different answer. Leo called Warden Robertson and suggested that he advise his guard to keep silent. The true outcome of this highly irregular "play rehearsal" would be determined at a meeting in the morning. Frances and Regina were closing up when Frank, Chuck, Jeannie, Wyatt, and Sylvia came into the waiting room. Wondering how much they knew, Frances and Regina just went about with their final tasks. Frank spoke first, "Nurse Frances, Lamar is on his way over from West Palm." No reaction from either of the girls, caused Wyatt to join in the fun, "Say, what's the name of the play, *'The Sock and the Chair?'*"

Frances, laughing loudly, addressed Frank, "Please tell me we were not on the news, and that you haven't called your parents, which would be worse than being on the news!"

It was Frank's turn to laugh, "No and no."

Chuck chimed in, "The news people looked deflated."

Jeannie could no longer control herself, "Someone heard the reporter grumbling that they'd dropped everything to run here and found themselves hoodwinked by a waylaid cast of Christians!"

Leo Gerehuazer came in and told Regina that her parents were on the way down with Lamar. "I think we need to send these two," presenting Frances and Regina, "to the middle east. We're wasting man power and weapons, when there would be certain surrender with these two ladies if they were armed with a sock, a car window, and a chair." Everyone was laughing, including the cast!

# Chapter Sixteen
# Seventy-Six Trombones

Dan walked into the clinic and hugged Regina and Frances tightly. He was highly concerned about what had occurred there earlier and what could happen as a result of it.

The whole group went out for pizza, including Leo and Hazel. Hazel was surprisingly upset, and voiced her opinion clearly. "Prisoners shouldn't be seen in the clinics." Elizabeth, close to tears, nodded in agreement. Regina spoke next, "The prisoner voluntarily hit the floor face down. Prisoners have never been a problem, but the overacting guards that escort them are another matter. Far more often than not they have been a source of disruptive antagonism, rather than the safety precaution that I assume they were intended to be.

Leo took his wife's hand and smiled at her, "Regina is right, and she and Frances have that place running like a top. The board can't believe the money that pours in steadily, because these two ladies care about what they do."

Salting his pizza, he continued, "a potential and <u>probable</u>

uproar was nipped in the bud today, as these two ladies worked quickly together, restraining  the guard, redirecting the patients and visitors, and consequently restoring immediate order. Quite frankly, I've never seen anything like it."

Grabbing the opportunity, Frances leaned forward, "She was assaulted by an armed prison guard in a public hospital clinic," smiling at Regina in admiration she continued, "and because of her immediate ingenious in handling the reporters, both facilities could walk away un-smeared."

"Not so fast, Nurse Frances," Regina interjected, "you were just as responsible for the media retreat as I was." The girls held up their glasses in a toast to each other.

Jeannie was the next speaker, "The funniest part of all is that everybody basically bought the explanation about the play!"

"The patients probably think that was the case, too," Wyatt shook his head and laughed.

Dan's soothing voice followed, "What happens now, Leo?"

"Well, tomorrow there is a big meeting in the conference room. Regina and Frances are in the position to press charges against the prison, which is essentially a charge against the city of Miami."

Lamar had fear in his voice, "Are they safe here? I think we should move both of them to West Palm Beach for a few days, while we think of a better idea."

Frances hugged Lamar, "There's no need to do that, honey, we're not in danger, they are."

"That's exactly why I think they should move," Lamar continued, "they don't always recognize danger, and when they do, it only intrigues them."

"What are your plans as far as charging the guard, girls?" Dan exhaled a very deep breath, as he comforted Elizabeth by squeezing her hand.

"I wasn't attacked; ask Pollyanna," Frances oddly appeared to be enjoying the prospective outcome.

All eyes were shifted to Pollyanna, who was tapping her straw as she silently prayed, "Father, please don't let them eat me alive, but this is our chance to get in and do Your work."

Almost shyly, she responded, "I would like to make a deal with them."

Frances clasped her hands together laughing, "I knew it!"

Frank, Chuck, Wyatt, Lamar, and Dan, simultaneously put their shaking heads in their hands, while Leo grinned.

Dan surfaced first, but knowing his little Pandemonium, he carefully chose his words, "What kind of a deal, honey?"

"For starters I would like to see the hospital establish a contract with the prison, that they refrain from interference when we are working with their inmates."

"They need to be entering through the back door, where the macho guards are upstaged by the mere delivery trucks," Frances added.

Sparkling, Regina continued, "If the city wants to sidestep a nasty publicity, I would like entrance to the prison weekly if not biweekly, to get to know the inmates and work with them."

Shaking heads involuntarily return to the hands, including

Leo's. "Regina," he smiled, "Warden Gordon doesn't like you; in fact, he hates you."

Frances stood up, "I like you Regina, and Warden Gordon has a lot to learn! I'm with you."

Jeannie and Sylvia also stood, both adding, "I'm with you too."

Hazel couldn't stand missing the excitement and pushed her chair back next, "Please count me in too."

The men were not only dumbfounded, but unhappy about this upcoming proposal and hoping in vain that it would fade away.

"Just what kind of work are you planning to do with the inmates, Miss Pollyanna and company?" Leo sounded concerned for the first time this evening.

The other men added input, causing a mass interrogation, followed by firm but gentle reprimands.

Waiting for attention she got it, and answered, "An enrichment program of some sort, and I would propose that we begin with an organized meeting with the inmates. We can't plan anything definite until we know who and what we are working with."

Leo was laughing and rubbing his eyes, "Let's see what the warden says in the morning. Mindy Thompson will talk to you girls in my office before the meeting."

Regina and Frances walked into the conference with their counsel, Mindy Thompson. Warden Robertson had his back to the three ladies, "That's the most ridiculous idea that I have ever heard," the warden shouted, waving a cigarette in the air as he spoke. "Your little lady lives in Never Land, Leo: pink castles, friendly dragons,

flying carpets, the whole nine yards. It's 'enough to gag a maggot.'"
Taking a long draw of his cigarette, he frowned as he exhaled.

"It may the only way to cover your butt," Melinda Thompson
was ready for action.

Leo introduced the three ladies as Melinda and Frances nodded coldly. Regina stepped forward extending her hand, which
the obligated warden shook only the fingers of.

The good looking grouch peered at Regina with the grayish-
blue eyes that could probably open a can of soup. The Board of
Directors was seated and the meeting began.

While everyone in the room except Regina and Frances dis-
agreed with the "offer," Melinda Thompson informed the group
that they might be wise to consider it. Warden Robertson sneered
at Regina and taunted, "Well now I've heard Snow White and the
Seven Dwarfs, Peter Pan, Cinderella, Sickeningly Sweet Regina
Brings Sunshine to Prison...."

To everyone's surprise Regina laughed heartily, and then
standing, she addressed the group, "My offer is final, with permission I'll excuse myself and return to clinic."

Frances stood next, "I'll join her, and I would like to add that
attacking someone who has the potential to fry your backside
may not serve you well, Warden."

Warden Robertson was ready to set fire to the army nurse.
He detested these ladies and wanted nothing to do with them.
Knowing that he was over a barrel, he realized that he would have
to work with them; but he vowed to make their little visits as mis-
erable as he could.

The girls went down to the clinic, planning their next move. "Mindy said to find out everything we can about the warden and that guard, so we can use it against them if we have to. What if he doesn't agree to work with us?" Regina was already disappointed.

"Warden Gordon isn't exactly in a position to call the shots since his guard screwed up royally, and he knows it. A suit against the city would be a reflection on his job, so let's assume they take our offer. What are you considering for the inmates as enrichment; any ideas?"

"I think we should split up into groups with each of us girls as information collectors. Let's make a short questionnaire and meet among ourselves afterward to compare notes."

"That sounds good, Pollyanna, and I've already contacted Public Relations to let them know that if this goes well, it will be a big plug for the hospital. They may send pizzas and sodas in for the meeting."

Dr. Gerehauzer walked in the door with a huge smile on his face. "Looks like you five ladies have a project to plan. Hazel is waiting to hear the outcome of the meeting, do you want to call her or should I? "

"We will," Frances answered, "what about the contract regarding prisoners being treated as patients here?"

"Melinda is drafting it, and the city officials are indebted to you ladies, or so they said."

Attempting to teach the "do-gooders" a fast lesson by overwhelming them, Warden Robertson called Leo to announce that in compliance with their "deal," he had lined up 76 inmates who were eligible for the enrichment program.

"Can they split them up into smaller groups for organization purposes?"

"NOPE!  Sorry Buddy, they wanted a task and now they've got one."

The warden had no inkling that a group of seventy six people was child's play to the ladies!

"Oh joy," Frank reacted sarcastically as he and Chuck sat down for their lunch.

"What do you girls hope to gain by this endeavor?" Chuck tipped back in his chair.

"Never mind, Polly, do you fellas intend to help us, or are you chickens after all?" Frances called their bluff. "And PUT THAT CHAIR DOWN, before you crack your skull."

"Well you're certainly not going to the prison alone at night, so I guess I'm in," Frank tried desperately to pretend that he was being forced.

"Ditto," Chuck answered. "I'll call Wyatt."

"Good then we'll have a task force of eight, we'll split up in pairs of two, you three couples and Hazel and I. Let's see, that will be two groups of 18 and two groups of 20, Tuesday's and Thursdays at 7:00. The first meeting will be pizzas and question-naires," Frances took quick notes.

"Questionnaires?" Chuck raised his eyebrows.

Regina answered, "Before we can plan anything, we need to

know the interests of the inmates we'll be dealing with. Once we get these, we'll all read the answers while we sort the information into groups that match."

Tuesday night arrived and the girls formed the four groups and had everyone introduced to each other before they realized what was going on. Pizza was catered in and the group ate it while filling out the questionnaires. Warden Robertson watched through the one way glass window, shaking his head in utter disgust. Returning to his office he saw a pizza box on his desk with a note: *Warden Robertson, we didn't know whether or not you've eaten. Regina.* Cold soda was left by the box, on a small pile of napkins. Locking his door, he ate the hot pizza, reassuring himself that she wouldn't know he did it.

Walking back to the meeting room he came in the door, as Regina immediately called the group to attention: "Ladies and gentlemen, let us take this opportunity to applaud Warden Robertson for allowing us the privilege we are enjoying." All stood and applauded, but the frustrated warden screamed at Regina, "Do you know what boundaries are, young lady?"

"I believe so, Sir."

"Then what made you think you had the right to enter my office?"

"I didn't, Sir. The guard at the desk did."

"Very well, he left the room, slamming the door behind him."

"Let's please resume our positions, so that we can get done," the un-ruffled missionary smiled.

The grateful inmates were exceptionally polite to the group

of missionaries. Complying with the safety guidelines that had been carefully set by Risk Management, all of them were serving time for non-violent crimes. Questionnaires in hand, Regina closed the meeting, and the new acquaintances exchanged respectful handshakes and departed.

The eight coordinators returned to Regina's to sort the data. The groups of interest were divided into four major categories: Art, Music, Dance, and other crafts/skills. Contrary to what the boys believed, they were stoked about the project, and had thoroughly enjoyed the first encounter.

Art- 9

Music – 38

Dance – 23

Crafts/skills – 6


Noteworthy characteristics:

Hank Riley – "Music Man, thief." Copped 83 wind instruments by scamming people.

Arthur Cadbury - Line dancing; square dancing; drill team experience!

Billy Rafter – "Draws like a banshee!"

Conner Cole – Enjoys wood working.

Elliott Uricks – Former tent maker.

All eight gathered around for what Regina called a win/win troubleshoot. Each person takes turns giving positive input and suggestions. Needless to say the guys had everyone in stitches –

"Hey we could have the tent maker build a covering for a flea market and sell the stuff that an organized group of thieves can gather from the other stands." Chuck

"Nice try, but we can't go out in public, especially to flea markets!" Frances

"We could form a dance team – the warden looks like he'd do a heck of a Fox Trot!" Frank

"Forget it!" Hazel

"Can we do anything with dancing?" Wyatt

"Limited, as we have no women." Regina

"We have five...." Chuck

"Forget it!" Frances, Regina, Jeannie, Sylvia, and Hazel

"WE COULD HAVE A BAND! A MARCHING BAND!" Frank

"How?" Wyatt

"We have 38 who like music – some even play instruments." Frank

"We have an experienced line dancer who also worked with high school drill teams!" Jeannie

"Tent maker, wood worker, and artist all spell flags to me!" Sylvia

"It sounds like a definite start, and a fairly good possibility." Frances

"Let's sleep on it, and have everyone get together with additional input." Regina

Frank took her wife in his arms and hugged her so tightly that he lifted her off the floor. Looking up at him, she asked, "How difficult is it to teach someone to play a band instrument?"

"Depends on the person and their musical ability; and that Riley guy said that he still owns the instruments he filched. He told Jeannie that they're in holding for him after he has served his time."

Lying in bed, Regina was talking to her beloved Abba, when Frank could not resist the opportunity to tease her, while praying, himself. Leaning over on one elbow, he gently shook her, "Hey, He's talking to me right now!" Releasing the feather pillow from under her head, Regina clocked him. Having custody of the pillow, Frank decided to keep it. "Give my pillow back," the tired redhead demanded. "No!" Frank continued to tease her. "Fine," said Regina pretending to reach for the phone. "Are you calling the police, Pollyanna?" he shook with laughter. "Not at all – I'm just calling your parents to tell them that you are working as a volunteer in the prison."

Frank couldn't stand it any longer; he was laughing when he returned the pillow, "Oh, my family's name! Please remember that if you ever do get tempted to call, that they'll be here within three hours!"

Warden Robertson opened the letter authorizing the conditional release of the stored instruments belonging to Hank Riley. Reaching for the phone in such haste that he almost tipped over his coffee, he cursed as he dialed Leo's number. "Leo, I was thinking that maybe we could substitute the electric chair for musical chairs. His voice was bitter as the sarcasm continued, "But with our Pollyanna and team of happy helpers why should anything in life be unpleasant?"

"Gordon, you need to stop looking for reasons to hate them."

"I need to start looking for another job! I carry a stomach distress bag every time there're here. That constant joy and oblivion makes my skin crawl!"

Because the prison was satisfying a debt by allowing Regina to carry on her work, the inmates were protected against retaliation from the staff. Eventually realizing this, they began to relax and openly enjoy the biweekly interactions with the outside world. In addition, the inmates were more respectful to the guards and to each other. When the huge crate of wind instruments was delivered to his office, the warden gave it an angry kick and sent for Hank Riley. The inmate appeared at the door with a guard, shaking with fear.

"Riley, here are the instruments for your temporary use." Opening the box, the inmate looked up for the next instruction. Staring at the mound of gold noisemakers, the warden shook his head, "We need an inventory of those and your signature."

"Yes Sir, of course," Hank's voice quivered.

Picking up a trumpet, the warden appeared be familiar with the instrument.

Nodding toward the horn, Hank said, "It suits you, Warden, did you ever play?"

Momentarily forgetting that he hated prisoners, the warden grumbled, "As a kid, but my father played the trumpet professionally."

The inventory continued in awkward silence. Hank Riley, deliberately leaving the trumpet on the warden's desk, returned the other instruments to the huge crate and watched as the maintenance men wheeled it to the group hall. He returned to his cell wondering how he would get in touch with God, if He really even existed.

Warden Robertson massaged his temples attempting to drone out the racket from a jackhammer across the street. So now there would be band instruments in his prison! What utter nonsense! He tried to soothe himself by picturing Regina Solberg being shot from a cannon into the fiery pit of hell, but instead, recalled his father playing the trumpet in the prominent orchestra in New York. Come to think of it he wasn't too bad himself at the horn. Seeing it on his desk, he picked it up and looked at it. Placing the gold instrument in the large bottom draw of his desk, he slammed it shut. He had work to do, and little Miss Sunshine was coming tonight.

The excitement was well controlled as the inmates were sorted into groups. Those who would be a drill squad, any who could play wind instruments, and percussion - to be started as soon as the donated instruments arrived. Three inmates could not read music but could draw a fairly good sound from the horns! Regina took them aside and spoke to them – "I will share a bit of scientific information with you, so listen carefully. The warden on the other side of the observation glass was all ears. "'According to recognized aerodynamics, the bumblebee cannot fly, due to the shape and weight of his body in relation to the total wing mass. But the bumblebee doesn't know this, so he goes ahead and flies anyway.'"

The three inmates were giving "Pollyanna" their undivided attention. "Now let's take the horns and play with them for a minute. Who knows the tune *Twinkle, Twinkle Little Star?"* All three nodded. "Oaky let's try it." With very little effort they had mastered the simple song. Before the end of the meeting they were blasting out *When the Saints Go Marching In*! Frank looked over at them and applauded. "You guys play by ear!" *"YOU GUYS PLAY BY EAR,"* the snooping warden mimicked to himself. The annoying witch left brownies on his desk this evening. When would she accept the fact that he despised her? Walking into the hall he brought the room to immediate attention. "I am calling a halt to this nonsense immediately!" he shouted.

Frances answered, "If that's your decision, Bucko, the bargain is off, and we all go back to the drawing board and sing like canaries." Startling everyone, he slammed the door as he left, shaking the one way glass almost hard enough to shatter it.

The missionaries were bursting with excitement when Hazel invited everyone back to her house for sandwiches. Leo was moved by what he heard, and shared the new information. "Tonight while you sun shiners were torturing Warden Gordon, I returned a message from Santo Cadaro, who works in Public Relations. Your percussion instruments are here, and they want to know if you need anything else!" Wyatt was making another sandwich, "A new door for the meeting hall or anger management classes for 'Bucko.'"

The band practices continued and were progressing rapidly. The inmates sounded great, the drill squad moved with precision, and the flags were coming along well. Organizing into their groups, the inmates prepared to start practice. The warden was in his office waiting for Regina to approach the guard at the desk with a "snack for him." He would take her head off right in front of him and hopefully wipe that sickening smile off her face. Opening his bottom drawer, he saw the trumpet and took it out. It was beautiful! There was a quiet knock on his door, which was unusual after office hours. Quickly placing the trumpet out of sight, he answered, "Come in."

The moon shot a ray of light through the window as Regina entered the office holding a large white bakery box. Approaching his desk she set it down and kissed him on the cheek. She turned quietly and left. Opening the box he saw a beautiful birthday cake with *Happy Birthday Warden Gordon* written on it.

The warden was speechless. Tears rolled down his cheeks, as he recovered the trumpet. He had forgotten that is was his birthday, as he had for the past many years.

Walking into the hall, he looked at the group of inmates, guards, and missionaries that stood respectfully before him. Bowing to Regina, he spoke,

"I wondered if this band needed another trumpet player, and if I might be considered for the job."

Regina burst into tears and ran into his arms. Frank, in tears himself, broke the touching moment into laughter, "Alright, Alright! Hands off my wife! First the sea captain, now a warden!"

Everyone hugged each other as Frank suggested that the warden, by all means play the trumpet, but also lead the band!

Warden Robertson would never be the same! "Madam Missionary," he began, "Surely you have some holy explanation for what has transpired here tonight!

Right now it's time to have cake, and we're late closing this meeting anyway, so we will expect it on Thursday."

"It will be on your desk, along with a SNACK!" Regina laughed.

"I'll have my snack in here with the rest of the band," he answered as everyone applauded.

Practices were outrageous! Warden Robertson was a fabulous musician! The inmates saw their warden in a different light, and respected him rather than fearing him. Returning the compliment, he viewed them as citizens who were making amends, rather than losers to be scoffed at and tormented. The music that poured from the band was incredible. While the flag was still a surprise, Regina was told that it was beautiful. Public Relations wanted a "public" performance, and the warden was not opposed! Positive publicity was one motive, but more importantly, the example of what can be done nationwide was another. The band, led by Warden Robertson, played Seventy Six Trombones and marched around the prison yard in practice. They also played God Bless America as a group, and When the Saints Go Marching In.

Business was still business at the prison, but on Tuesday and Thursday nights, business was music. Missionary music!

# Chapter Seventeen
# Encore!

The next meeting in the JMH conference room was much different than the one of six months prior. Melinda Thompson could not believe that the man who shook her hand was the same Warden Robertson. His receptive demeanor was the first curve thrown, and the man she'd met prior had grayish eyes, while his appeared to be a bright blue. Introducing himself as Gordon Robertson, and explaining the details of a public presentation, he charmed the Board of Directors, the department of Public Relations, and Risk Management. Speaking highly of Regina and Frances, he closed his speech with the words, "Mrs. Solberg and Mrs. McNeal have brought new hope to those who had lost all hope. Together with the rest of their team, they have changed anger into music, hatred into understanding, and bitter rivalry into teamwork. They did these things with the power of God, in Whom I do believe.

In six weeks the prison band, now known as *The Musical Cons*, would perform live at the Miami Convention Center at 7:00 pm.

Tickets were selling at such a ridiculous speed that there was talk that they may need two performances. The city officials were ecstatic over the potential income and grand publicity for Miami. Under the guidance of the warden, himself, uniforms that were designed by Sylvia and Jeannie were being made in red, white and blue, and the flag which was being done in the group that was headed by Frances and Hazel, was finished, although Regina was told that she couldn't see it until the performance! Frank worked with the wind instruments while Chuck and Wyatt coordinated percussion. Regina worked with the drill team.

Both families were invited to the show, and since Frank and Regina Solberg were praised to high heavens in the paper, and had JMH backing, the Solbergs were not too difficult to deal with! The large group had arranged to sit together for practicality, as they had all been invited to the gala reception following the performance. Everyone was dressed in semi-formal attire and the group seemed honored to be included. Dan, who was beaming with pride had his camera ready, while Raymond checked his pocket for Kleenex. Bub and Sis chatted nervously with Andrea, as the two mothers were tersely polite. Elizabeth wore a black beaded "I'm more appropriately dressed than you are" suit, with a matching evening bag, and taffeta heels. Dorothy sported an orange and yellow Indian printed long dress that hung five inches from the floor, with "now I'm really bigger than you," three inch high cloth pumps. Sis and Andrea were in smart cocktail dresses, and the three men wore dark suits. Dorothy leaned over to talk to Andrea, "I hope your sister is properly dressed; you know the press will be here!" Andrea smiled and resisted the temptation to ask her sister's mother-in-law where she purchased the flood dress, as Dan winked approvingly.

Lamar and Leo were seated among the group of eight missionaries in the front row. The men all wore black suits and the ladies had beautiful evening dresses. Regina wore a pale green crepe dress and matching shoes. Her hair fell loosely around her shoulders in thick bouncy curls. Frank looked proud with her on his arm as they walked to the front row. Dorothy was covering her annoyance well, but Dan still noticed it. She was the matriarch of the Solberg family and did not appreciate the attention that Regina seemed to generate everywhere she went.

Opening the show, The Musical Cons Marching Band, led by Warden Gordon Robertson, played the National Anthem followed by God Bless America. They continued to wow the audience with Seventy-Six Trombones, When the Saints Go Marching In, and Tie a Yellow Ribbon. The drill team added to the excitement as the crowd went wild. The band took a bow but in response to the shouting, "ENCORE!" they reassembled. After another song, Gordon Robertson took the microphone. "Ladies and Gentlemen, I would like to share something with you tonight. In the midst of the organization of our band, a little missionary who was a VERY BIG PROBLEM for our prison caused a bright light to seep into our walls and remain there. I asked her for an explanation, which she agreed to have on my desk forty-eight hours later. Two days followed, and when I walked into my office I found her interpretation, right on schedule. This is what the report said:

"Warden Robertson, here is the only explanation that I have. It was written by Myra Brooks Welch, and describes your scenario perfectly!"

'Twas battered and scarred, and the auctioneer
Thought it was scarcely worth while
To waste any time on the old violin,
But he held it up with a smile.
"What am I bidden, good folks," he cried,
"Who'll start the bidding for me?"
"A dollar, a dollar;" then, "Two! Only two?"
"Two dollars, and who'll make it three?"
"Three dollars once; three dollars, twice;
Going for three" - But no,
From the back of the room, a gray-haired man
Came forward and picked up the bow;
Then, wiping the dust from the old violin,
And tightening all the loose strings,
He played a melody pure and sweet,
As a caroling angel sings.

The music ceased, and the auctioneer,
With a voice that was quiet and low,
Said: "What am I bid for the old violin?"
As he held it up with the bow.
"A thousand dollars, and who'll make it two?
Two thousand! And who'll make it three?
Three thousand once; three thousand twice,
And going, and gone," said he.
The people cheered but some of them cried,
"We do not quite understand,
What changed it's worth." Swift came the reply,

"The touch of a master's hand."
And many a man with life out of tune,
And battered and scarred with sin,
Is auctioned cheap to a thoughtless crowd,
Much like the old violin.
A "mess of pottage," a glass of wine;
A game- and he travels on.
He is "going" once, and "going" twice,
He's "going" and almost "gone."
But the Master comes, and the foolish crowd,
Never can quite understand;
The worth of a soul and the change that's wrought,
By the touch of the Master's hand.

"Ladies and gentlemen, at this time I would like to call Frank and Regina Solberg up here. Two band members have created our flag, and we would like to present it at this time. Billy Rafter and Elliott Uricks came forward with a beautiful flag displaying a painting of a gray-haired man holding an old violin, above the name: "The Musical Cons Marching Band." Regina felt the tears coming and did not try to stop them. Addressing the audience again, the warden spoke, "We have a special gift for Mrs. Solberg and a very special guest this evening. At his request, it is my pleasure to call Mr. Irving Berlin to present the award."

Irving Berlin came out as the crowd jumped to their feet applauding. He handed Regina a small velvet box. She opened it to find a gold necklace supporting a little charm of an old violin. It was crafted by the inmates, all of whom loved her. Frank placed the necklace around her neck as the crowd continued to applaud.

Warden Robertson addressed the audience again, "The light that Mrs. Solberg helped us discover, still shines in the prison, and I would be willing to bet my stolen trumpet, that it always will."

Frank was presented with a beautiful award from JMH, School of Medicine, and the other six tireless workers received awards of special recognition from the  city of Miami. The exhausted crowed enjoyed three more songs by The Musical Cons, before the show came to an end, or rather, a beginning!

The huge reception followed the show, which the warden asked the security stay over and escort the inmates to. "I know that Regina would really like to be with them tonight." Shocked city officials questioned his orders by saying, "Socialization of this nature is highly irregular." The warden answered, "There is little about Regina Solberg that is not highly irregular! Just stick around, and you'll see!"

Both families were delighted to meet and socialize with Irving Berlin, and the band. Their stories were both entertaining and touching. Melinda Thompson and Warden Robertson also enjoyed the evening together, laughing about the misjudged first impressions that each originally had about the other.

The Musical Cons were to continue as a group, under the direction of their respected warden, with the eight founders overseeing things! Regina had gotten to know all of the people at the prison, and she was deeply fond of them. She was still surprised to see Wallace Hanley, the guard who had thrown her into the wall, crying. He walked toward her and reached in his pocket. "I have a gift for you, it's just from me. It was a very small figure of a gorgeous Infant. His beautiful face had sad little tears on it, and His blanket said, "no matter how much you hurt Me, I'll still love you." The guard could hardly speak, "Regina, can you ever forgive me?" She hugged him and whispered, "You're too late! I did that months ago!" Nodding at the little Baby, he added, "I hope someday, He can." Regina looked into his eyes, "Do you believe that I have forgiven you?"

"Why yes, sure I do."

"Do you think I'm better than God?" she smiled gently.

The group of missionaries was up all night celebrating, and they all seemed to know that the Master among them was smiling the whole time!

# Chapter Eighteen
# Great Expectations!

Although it was barely May, the weather sprinted toward summer, spiking temperatures and displaying early signs of humidity. It hardly seemed possible that the third year of medical school was ending. Sylvia was having a grand party next week to celebrate the completion of Wyatt's residency, and the opening of his new practice on Coral Way.

Frances and Lamar announced their engagement, and he would be retiring and moving to Miami. His son, Brian Mac Michaels, would be joining Dan as the new junior partner. The six-pack, which had recently become the ten-pack, continued to seize any excuse to have a party, and enjoyed it to the hilt! With Lamar moving to the city, he and Leo could console each other while their wives enjoyed the pickles that the three younger girls seemed to tumble upon regularly.

This Saturday morning, Hazel and Frances were planning the upcoming June wedding, while Sylvia, Jeannie and Regina had just left the airport. Hyacinth and Roger were arriving from Jamaica to liven the festivities!

The entire ten pack and the two visitors would meet for lunch at the Doral Country Club, where Leo and Lamar were finishing a golf game.

As the greetings circulated, the group noticed that Sylvia was glowing; but it was Hyacinth who recognized the underlying reason. "You not just hoppy because Wyatt gra-du-Wait-tin. I suspect dare's more to it den dat?"

Just before lunch, Wyatt and Sylvia joined hands and confirmed her mother's suspicion. The new addition to the Clement family would be arriving in seven months. Everyone was teary eyed with joy, as Lamar raised his hands, "That baby will have more people doting on him than the royals in England!" Roger, who never said anything laughed hard, "Dat poor baby gonna hove more grand Pair-Ents den he know what to do wit!" Frank and Regina were asked to be the godparents and hugs surrounded the table, as the tolerant waitress stood out of the way. Drink orders were taken and the happy gang moved in on the huge buffet that included a dessert table with twenty three selections of its' own.

After lunch the group went in separate directions allowing Sylvia and Wyatt to take the tired travelers home for a rest. The Gerehauzers and the future Mac Michaels went to see the chapel that would house the wedding ceremony, and the Nugents and the Solbergs went to the pool at Isla Del Mar. Everyone would gather later for an evening cookout, and to continue organizing the upcoming festivities.

Jeannie and Regina were chatting with excitement, as there

were two showers, a wedding, and a christening coming up, and there wasn't a moment to lose.

Chuck and Frank were not ruling out the possibility that their own wives were also ready to "play dolls" with Sylvia. Chuck brought the subject up first, "You know that our ladies want babies, too?"

"Regina already tries to kidnap any child that strays more than eighteen inches from the parents!"

"Well, that's what they have student loans for, and Jeannie could still work part time."

"Heck yeah, look at all of our classmates that have kids who are already toddlers."

The evening was filled with excitement and planning. Frank would be back on the hand service for the summer and Chuck was scheduled to do histories and physicals. Frances and Lamar loved the chapel which was close to the Doral, so the reception would be held at the country club where they had all just eaten lunch a few hours ago. Lamar surprised Frances with a new house on the Doral Golf Course, which would undergo slight remodeling right after the closing of the sale.

Frances and Hazel were like sisters and the three younger women looked up to them. Regina loved seeing Frances, who was like a second mother to her, so happy. Likewise, she had always loved Dan's business partner. The union of the two of them and the wonderful news that they would be living in Miami was an overwhelming wave of happiness. Lamar had told Dan, "I can't take Frances from Miami, Regina is there!"

Clinic hours flew by and in spite of the heat outside, everyone seemed lighthearted and relatively carefree. Warden Robertson popped in to say hello, on his way back from having lunch with Mindy Thompson. The couple had been seeing each other since the prison band formed. Frances and Regina both wondered why neither of them had ever married. "Well I can understand sour puss Gordon being single, since he just recently became human," Frances mumbled, "but Mindy is sweet, smart, and good looking." "I think that Mindy had her heart shattered years ago, when her fiancée left her at the altar. She  never really pursued another relationship, until the last meeting upstairs with Gordon," Regina shared news that she'd  overheard. "Oh, well that will do it. It would for me. It did for me. My husband-to-be returned from the war married to somebody else."

"Ahhh," Regina nodded in thought, "Well that's his big loss, wherever he may be."

June approached and the wedding shower that was given by the other four women in the "top ten," was fantastic. The party was at the Gerehauzers, and  Regina's family had been invited among the other guests. The men were out on the patio talking about golf, while the ladies chattered happily inside. The honored couple got beautiful gifts and both the bride and groom-to- be, looked decades younger than they were.

The wedding was small but elegant. Frances looked stunning in a silk, ivory, tea-length dress with a deeply scalloped neckline. Her hair was beautifully done in an upsweep and she wore small pearl drop earrings to match the simple strand necklace that had belonged to her mother. Lamar wore a dark suit and Dan matched him as his best man. Hazel was the Matron of Honor, and wore a simplification of Frances's dress in a pale blue. During the reception Jeannie and Regina caught each other's eye and went into the ladies lounge. Simultaneously they said, "I have to tell you something," and both burst out laughing. "You first," Regina smiled, "what do you have to tell me?"

Jeannie was bubbling with excitement, "I'm pregnant!" The two girls hugged and cried. Regina, blotting her face with a Kleenex, added, "Me too!"

Again at the same time, "Does Frank/Chuck know?" Laughing uncontrollably both confessed that they just found out and didn't have a chance to tell them yet. They plotted a scheme to announce the news at home, and opened the door to return to the reception. Frank and Chuck took one look at their wives and nodded. Both men had seen pregnancy tests in their homes earlier, but hadn't let on.

As the celebration continued, Dan was dancing with Regina and commented, "Honey, you look beautiful, I've never seen you look happier." Regina hugged him tightly. She loved her stepfather, and the two had always shared a close bond. Andrea similarly commented, but Regina wanted Frank to know before everyone else. Frances was dancing with Chuck and hinted, "Don't you think Jeannie looks unusually happy tonight?" Chuck smiled but didn't answer, "And Regina? She looks happy too. One of them is pregnant!" Chuck hugged Frances and told her that he and

Frank had both seen test kits but knew nothing yet. "You are the Honorable Charles Nugent, are you not? You and Frank should call them out on this matter."

"What if they don't want anyone to know yet?" the tempted "judge" asked. "Then they shouldn't be cavorting to the ladies room and coming out glowing. One of them if not both are guilty of withholding information."

"Well, we do have evidence. Do you want to have some fun?"

"Right here and now!" Regina's second mother was beaming.

Chuck pulled Frank aside and the plan was instantaneous. Frank walked up to the bandleader and borrowed the microphone. "Order in the court," he said seriously. "The Honorable Charles Nugent, posing." The guests laughed as Frances came forward, "Your Honor, several of us have reason to believe, beyond the shadow of a doubt, that Jeannie Marie Nugent and Regina Louise Solberg, are guilty of withholding information." Jeannie stood, in her place, "I'm entitled to an attorney," she laughed. Chuck displaying unbelievable self restraint answered, "Young lady, you have laughed in my court. You are entitled to nothing." Indicating Regina, the poser continued, "Mrs. Solberg, how do you plead?"

"I don't mind going to jail, Your Honor, I hear the music is great!" Frank walked over to her and took her in his arms, "Which of you is pregnant?"

"I cannot say at this moment."

"Okay both of you ladies, come up here and sit before the judge." Two chairs were brought up as Frank continued, "Your

Honor, here they are." Chuck took over, "The party who is pregnant will kindly stand. Both girls stood as their husbands kissed them. "Grandchildren! We'll have three grandchildren!" Frances clasped her hands together, as Lamar hugged her.

Sylvia stood shyly and spoke softly, "I beg to correct the witness, Your Honor, but they will not have three." Everyone grew deathly quiet. "They will have five, she laughed!" Wyatt was thrilled to have the recent news announced. Regina and Jeannie went to her and hugged her. "Triplets!" they cried together. Chuck and Frank turned pale – "I hope that's not contagious," the future Dr. Solberg stuttered, and the poser judge looked a little faint as well.

The party ran overtime, as nobody wanted it to end. Leo Gerehauzer approached Chuck and said, "Your Honor, I need a court order stating that Regina Solberg cannot leave the Department of Orthopedics!" Regina hugged him. "I won't, I still have to work. Just give me a few hours off to have my baby." Dan, put his arms around Regina and answered, "Now wait a minute, Leo, the Indians get to miss one row of corn; so I think the Italians should compete with that record."

"It's settled then," Leo laughed, "you get half an hour off." Hazel and Frances shook their heads, as Jeannie spoke, "It's obvious that men do not have babies. Sylvia, maybe you can get ninety minutes off!" It appeared that the lives of the top ten were not going to be placid for many years to come, if ever!

The three pregnant ladies were walking on air, and Sylvia, who was just starting her second trimester, was a great resource of guidance for the other two. Dreading the call to the Solberg seniors, Regina prayed for help, "Abba, thank you for this ultimate gift of pure joy. Please help me to treat my in-laws with kindness and understanding, so that we may all celebrate this miracle together!" Frank rolled his eyes as Dorothy gave him a list of demands and conditions.

1.  Regina was to see a doctor immediately and make her medical records available to the family.

2.  She was to have the baby at JMH where Frank was.

3.  She was to allow the Solbergs to interview, hire, and supervise, a nanny or quit her job before the end of the third trimester.

4.  She was to research a proper environment for the nursery and allow the Solbergs to hire a decorator to meet the standards found.

When Frank hung up the phone, he was livid, but Regina was laughing. "They have no right to make any of those demands, honey, and no doctor will release any information to them."

"We are going to have another feud, I can feel it."

"We never had a first feud. They huffed and puffed and wound up blowing their own little house down."

"I don't need you to be under any stress from them, Regina, you are carrying our baby."

"We'll just ignore the demands and see what happens."

Both Jeannie and Sylvia were having their babies at Trinity Hospital, an exclusive private facility conveniently located near the Doral. When her ultrasound revealed triplets, Sylvia was transferred to JMH for the continuation of care, for safety precautions. JMH had one of the finest neonatal units in the country, and Wyatt felt more comfortable there. Jeannie hated JMH and was staying where she was, and Regina also opted for Trinity. Both girls had appointments with Dr. Richard Young, an obstetrician just out of residency.

Jeannie had the first appointment in a week and Regina would go in two weeks.

Before her appointment came up, Regina was rushed to the emergency room for acute pain which turned out to be kidney stones. Frances was in tears, and begged her to switch her case to JMH. Regina agreed so that Frances would relax. Walking out of the emergency room, she saw the senior Solbergs waiting. When they saw Frances they stood up to go inside. Frances was in no mood to beat around the bush. "I'll tell you two right now, that Regina has now been labeled high risk. That means you limit your conversations to other things besides this pregnancy. You will ask her no questions, and you will make no demands or even suggestions. Is that clear?" The Solbergs were both dumbfounded, but it was Dorothy who answered. "Listen Frances, we make rules because we love those kids." "They are not kids," she snapped, –"They are having a kid. It is not your place to interfere, and any stress you create could harm your grandchild. Now sit your backsides down because you will not be seeing Regina until she comes out. The emergency room is not a social club."

Frances walked to the desk and called Dr. Andrew Kingsley, a prominent obstetrician from the United Kingdom, and an attending at JMH. Head of the High Risk Department, he was a middle aged man with a thick British accent.

Tall and stocky, he had black hair, a closely trimmed beard and handsome green eyes. He had known Frances for years and was very fond of her. When she explained Regina's situation, he left his office and came to the emergency room.

"Regina, I'm Andrew Kingsley, it's lovely to meet you." Regina was relieved when he assured her that no harm could have come to the baby and that she would need to be very careful with her diet as the stones were calcium based. He walked her out of the emergency room as both the Solbergs, pushed passed Frank to get to him. "Dr. Kingsley, may I introduce myself, I'm - "

"Not pregnant judging by your age, Madame! You needn't introduce yourself to me unless you are the patient." Winking at Frank, he observed the crowd of people waiting to see his new patient. Frank hugged Regina and asked her what she wanted to do about dinner.

"You can go home and rest, which would probably be wise."

"It's whatever you want, princess," added Leo with tears in his eyes.

"I'm fine," Regina answered.

"That is the understatement of the century," Dr. Kingsley added in a crisp British accent.

Dorothy blurted out again, as Dan concealed a laugh. "Andy, she must not have any excitement."

The irritated attending straightened, "I don't see an Andy, and let's not confuse excitement with aggravation. You, Madame, appear to be a source of the latter."

Jeannie turned away laughing and Regina could have hugged him.

Dan proceeded with caution, "Dr. Kingsley, is it safe to take Regina out to dinner?"

Leo stepped toward them, "Andrew, this is Dan McBride, Regina's father."

Shaking his hand, "Andrew Kingsley, It's a pleasure to meet you. I don't think Regina will be rattled by dinner. She seems to be a solid little lady."

Goliath, prepared with a paper and pen, shoved her way forward again to get into the doctor's direct line of vision. "What are Regina's diet restrictions, Andrew?"

"They're none of your damn business!" Frances move quickly toward her, intercepted by a restraining hug from Lamar.

Andrew Kingsley laughed and then, answered slowly and clearly, "I would suggest that we all recognize Regina as a very capable adult. Where is that blasted sock, by the way?" He raised his eyebrows at the blushing redhead. Regina looked at Sylvia who was laughing. She and Regina now had the same physician, and he had been informed during a second ultrasound, of how they'd all met and become the top ten.

Dorothy, unabashed, suggested Melody Inn, as a quiet place to dine. The top ten and the four West Palm Beach arrivals ate together peacefully. Frank had intended to inform his parents to back off, but realized that Andrew Kingsley and Frances beat him to it.

# Chapter Nineteen

# The "King and I," vs. The Hospital and You

The hot summer was coming to an end and the three pregnant ladies were delighted to see it go! Sylvia, who looked like a model for maternity clothes, was especially relieved, as she carried three times the weight as the others. Regina was not yet showing, which did not please her in the least, and the upcoming Nugent was barely visible. "Just wait," Sylvia counseled, "you'll show soon enough."

Jeannie and Sylvia were extremely cautious patients, and a delight for their doctors to deal with. Regina on the other hand was not. She didn't like doctors and randomly skipped appointments unless they were necessary by her standards. Andrew Kingsley came to the clinic and asked Frances, "Am I supposed to break my arm or leg to see my patient?"

"She looks and feels great, Andrew."

"Wonderful! I would like to have the chance to write that in her chart."

Coming out of a room, Regina saw him. "Dr. Kingsley, how nice to see you!"

"Mrs. Solberg, it would be nice to see you too!"

Laughing and blushing at the same time, "Did I miss another appointment?"

"Indeed."

Frances saved the day, as usual, "Andrew, you should try her turkey salad sandwiches."

"Is that an invitation?"

"Certainly," Regina answered handing him a plate from her cart.

"That is absolutely delicious," the British attending, took a sip of lemonade.

"We call this lunch at Pollyanna's," Frances informed him.

"Well according to my recollection, Pollyanna did as she was instructed, especially by a doctor!" He responded, trying to sound convincing.

"Point taken, Doctor," Regina was always charming when necessary.

"Very well then, I'll see you next week." Andrew smiled as he walked toward the door.

Sylvia waited patiently for her name to be called by Dr. Kingsley's receptionist, who could be very curt. "Mrs. Clements, we will take you back now, and please try to ask the doctor any questions that you may have at this time, rather than calling numerous times during the week." Nearly in tears, Sylvia shook her head, "I must excuse myself for a minute, I'll reschedule." Waiting for the elevator door to close, she began to cry and went to Orthopedics to see Frances. "Well that was an unnecessary remark for any receptionist to make, and Andrew wouldn't appreciate that one bit. Come on, honey, let's go back together."

"I can't," Sylvia snubbed, "I've missed my appointment."

"We'll see about that," The army nurse was resurrecting!

Approaching the desk, Frances asked to see Dr. Kingsley.

"Do you have an appointment?" The snippy lady asked, eying Sylvia.

"Do you have any sense?" Frances answered, walking right passed her.

When Frances explained what happened, Andrew was furious. Sylvia spoke quietly, "I do call too much, Doctor, but I'm scared as this is my first pregnancy."

"If I may be so bold," Andrew spoke slowly, "You are also carrying triplets."

"Yes," She answered shyly.

"I like to talk to my patients, and I will certainly talk to the receptionist. By the way, I wish your little redheaded friend would do us the honor of dropping by once in awhile. Do you know if she was thwarted by Miss Congeniality as well?"

Laughing, Sylvia answered, "If Regina wasn't thwarted by a stone cold warden, I doubt that a receptionist could sway her!"

"Well then I'll leave her to you, Frances," he smiled.

"I'm a nurse, not a magician." She answered. "Regina is resistant to doctors; I'm surprised she married one!"

Coming in with the groceries, they heard the telephone ringing. Frank scooped Monique up, set a full bag of produce on the table, and answered the call. Regina added the finishing touches to the pot roast dinner in the crock pot as she listened. "Well, wait a minute, is that a done deal? Well, you should have asked us first! Sure the extra space would be wonderful, but Regina is a high risk pregnancy and we don't need to move."

Regina answered the door to find Chuck and Jeannie with Dodger. "Come in, my dears, show time is just beginning," she laughed nodding toward the phone. Hanging up with unusual force, Frank threw his hands in the air, and sat down on the couch.

"What's up, brother," Chuck couldn't wait to hear this one.

"My parents have rented our apartment and purchased the three bedroom unit that was for sale upstairs. They want us to move."

Jeannie and Regina were thrilled. "Now you'll have a room for the baby!" Jeannie hugged her friend.

"Now we'll be on the same floor," Regina hugged her back.

"Now my parents will spend the night when they come," Frank looked like he was ready to throw up.

"Negative," Chuck reassured, "make it an office and don't put a bed in it."

"Regina doesn't need a move right now, do you, honey?"

"Worse things could happen," she smiled.

"They have put the three bedroom in our names too, IF we manage this apartment for them, we will own both WHEN I graduate, IF I do a residency here."

Chuck was doubled over, "IF someone doesn't shoot them first, THEN you'll own both anyway!"

Frank was still shaking his head as Regina and Jeannie were

planning the new nursery. The two girls had just finished helping Sylvia with hers which was done in nursery rhymes. Jeannie's was started in a small animal farm, and Regina had planned a one wall mini circus, but now she could go all out with it. Dorothy had settled down a little, realizing that if she didn't, she could be completely left out. She made no further mention of her original requirements, and told Regina that her doctor was a rude, conceited, snob. Regina had learned to become a very good listener, and said little in response.

The two couples walked upstairs to the three bedroom unit, which was unlocked and being cleaned. It was lovely and the nursery was huge. It was two doors down from Chuck and Jeannie, which delighted the two girls even more.

"Don't sweat the move, Frank," his friend consoled, "we'll all get together and have it done in a few hours." Regina and Jeannie conned the boys into finishing the pot roast dinner while they ran out to Diamonds. "They have bright colored fabric for twenty-five cents a yard!" Regina pictured the curtains.

"And it will be gone before we know it," Jeannie wanted to bash Franks parents, and had been cautioned by Chuck that it may be best not to comment too much.

Regina called her in-laws to thank them for the new place. When asked about the nursery, she chose her words carefully. "We want the baby to have a bright and stimulating setting, and yet a child friendly one. Frank and Adam are both brilliant and I have no reason to believe that your grandchildren wouldn't take after them."

Was it morning sickness Regina was feeling, or this conversation that should have been accompanied by a shovel?

"Well that is very sweet, dear," Dorothy bought the pitch. "But you will need help, and I don't want Frank stressed with decorating."

"Of course not and I don't either; there are people on the campus at the National Center for Child Development. I will call on them." There were, and she would! She would call to say hello while decorating the nursery as she pleased!

"Well I'm glad to hear that you can be sensible, Regina."

"Please let us know who you spoke with and what they said."

"Of course," *when pigs knit sweaters,* she thought to herself, hanging up.

The five men from the ten-pack were plotting for a change! There was a dinner theater in Ft. Lauderdale where Yul Brenner would be performing live in the beloved, *King and I.* Leo had six tickets donated by the Public Relations Department, and he knew just who could use them! The six younger "kids" could have the tickets and the two older couples could pay their way in. He moved quickly to be sure they could get seats together, and then called Wyatt to insure his call coverage. Frank and Chuck were thrilled, as both their wives adored Yul Brenner. Regina in particular had loved the actor since she was seven years old and had seen the performance on the big screen.

Everyone in the large group looked forward to the following Saturday night. Dressing for the show, Regina doubled over with the familiar pain that had been diagnosed as a probable stag horn calculus kidney stone. Since she had strictly refused X-ray exploration, the consulting physicians could only make an educated guess. Andrew Kingsley had gone round after round with her about the necessity of an X-ray, and been defeated every time by his stubborn patient. "No X-rays, especially during the first trimester!" Regina had said it over and over again.

"We must have an answer," Andrew had argued.

"Ultrasound gave us an answer; they said it's a probable stag horn calculus stone. That makes sense but X-ray does not."

"Is that so? Perhaps you should put your name on the door! I thought this was MY practice."

"I thought this was MY baby."

"You need to do some thinking, Regina."

"I am thinking. About all of the poor babies in the world that will be lost just because you're not their doctor!"

"Get a new doctor," Andrew shouted tossing her chart into the trash can.

Seeing her cover her face and the watching the small shoulders quiver, Andrew walked toward the table. As he placed a gentle hand on her shoulder, his face grew red with anger. He did not appreciate this little brat laughing so hard that she couldn't speak.

"I'm telling OSHA what you did to my chart."

"Just get out!"

"With ple-shaw," she mocked his British accent.

They had sorted the misunderstanding out the next day in Orthopedics. Regina did not need another fight with him, but she did call to report the incident as she had promised to do. "Come to the hospital now, Regina. I'm here on call, and you can see me in the emergency room."

"I can also see Yul Brenner, and that's where I'm going."

"Regina, I am warning you. If you do not present yourself within the hour, I will drop your case. You are getting an X-ray, whether you like the idea or not!"

"Make room for another patient, because I'm going to see Yul Brenner. Besides, the ultrasound already confirmed the diagnosis."

"Where's Frank, I want to talk to him!"

"Souls in hell want ice water. Good-bye."

Regina, called the best Doctor there was, "Father, I want to go to the play. Yul Brenner is terminally ill and I'll never get this chance again. Andrew is also in one of his moods, and I don't want to see him. Could You please stay by me and get me through this once again?"

Dinner was a rack of lamb accompanied by sweet baby carrots, scalloped potatoes, a wonderful salad, and chef's bread. The dessert was carrot cake and coffee. The performance was sensational! Yul Brenner was even more spectacular than Regina remembered from many years ago, and the entire evening was a memory that all of them would cherish forever. After the play ended, Yul Brenner came back on stage again in response to the second standing ovation, and threw his arms high in the air as the audience cheered louder.

Regina eventually passed the stone late in the night and made brief notes for her next doctor. Frank was concerned about her and asked her to call Andrew. "I spoke with him earlier, Frank, and the same old fight continued. He wants me to get a new doctor, and that's fine with me."

"Regina," Frank sounded stern, "That's not fine at all."

"Nobody is going to convince me to do anything that I feel could hurt the baby."

"Andrew is not going to advise you to do anything that will hurt the baby."

"Andrew isn't always right, either. The ultrasound technician told me he wouldn't use radiation if it was his child, especially since the test confirmed what they suspected."

"May I please call him?"

"The ultrasound technician? Sure, go ahead."

"Andrew, Regina! May I please call Andrew?"

"If you intend to be his patient! I am leaving JMH, and going back to Trinity, Frank, and that's final."


Regina finished painting the Paper Mache' clown she had made for the nursery. The large figure was holding a bunch of balloons designed to look like he was floating down from the sky by them. In the other hand, he held a small wooden box marked, "hot dogs," with three tiny Steiff toy canines in it, preserved from Frank's childhood. The clown would be supported by fishing line on a hook in the ceiling hidden by the brightly colored big top!

The tightrope unicyclist, also suspended by fishing line, pedaled across the room, on a colored rope fastened to the side walls. A large stuffed elephant sat on a trapeze that hung just low enough to hold wipes, while another pair of Mache'clowns busied themselves above the changing table, stacking diapers.

A sturdy wooden popcorn wagon on wheels, which was designed and painted by Frank, stood in one corner. He had positioned the intricate Mache' contents to look like they were actually popping and falling into a mound of buttery puffs. The top of the cart was a practical shelf, displaying adorable children's books. Two cotton candy salesmen posed by the windows, were smiling and holding their wares in boxes suspended by shoulder straps. The delicately tinted, pink cotton cones in their trays looked realistic enough to eat. Regina had used several dolls from her extensive collection to make the setting spring to life. Frank was proud of his wife, but he worried about her day and night. Her unique creativity reflected from every scene in his unborn baby's new room, and he loved her beyond description. He prayed constantly that her delivery would be safe and that their baby would be well.

As they were putting the finishing touches on the mural of the crowd, Chuck and Jeannie came to the door. Both were amazed at the nursery! Frank was glad to see his friend, and shared the problem with Andrew, while the girls looked at the big top. Chuck was deeply concerned, but tried not to worry his friend. "Andrew is a magnificent doctor, Frank, but he is used to women like Sylvia. His patients literally take notes when he talks to them. A non-compliant patient like Regina, is bound to rock his world."

"So what do I do? She refuses to go back to him."

"Why? What happened?"

"They had another big argument yesterday afternoon, and he ordered her to come to the hospital. Regina wouldn't miss seeing Yul Brenner to comply with a threatening gunman!"

"I'd let Andrew handle it. It's his job to deal with his patients, whether they are married to house staff or not."

Sylvia and Wyatt came over with a pan full of conch fritters, and the six of them ate on the patio. Wyatt and Sylvia raved about the nursery, and told Regina that *The Miami Herald* should do an article on it.

The three girls were setting out brownies and ice cream, when the subject of Andrew came up. Sylvia gasped, as she was very intimidated by her charming obstetrician. Jeannie was not one bit surprised, but agreed with Regina about the X-ray. "What will you do now?" Sylvia still could not believe that her friend had hung up on Andrew. "Find another doctor at Trinity," Regina seemed more concerned with the last polka dot on her drying clown.

The next morning in clinic, Leo was waiting for her. "Pollyanna," he started in his harshest army voice, "Are you trying to give Dr. Kingsley a heart attack?"

"Sir, No Sir," she responded smiling, "I'm trying to give my baby the best chance that I can."

"Sweetheart, you need to be followed here by the high risk specialists."

"Well Mr. High Risk, is on his high horse, and I'm tired of his threats."

Leo desperately tried to suppress a laugh, but could hold it no longer. He hugged Regina, and continued, "You do have the right and responsibility to think decisions through, whether any doctor likes it or not. Typically, high risk patients are anxious, but they usually tend to be over compliant rather than non-compliant."

"Well, he dropped my case, and I'm glad."

"Andrew would never drop your case, honey."

Andrew had come in the door at the beginning of Leo's sentence. "That's absolutely correct."

"You promised!" Regina looked disappointed.

"I was frustrated, Regina. You are the most difficult patient that I have ever had."

"Then you are one lucky doctor, and you should thank God for your good fortune."

"Will you return to my office? I know we can come to some agreement."

"No."

Frances had been listening intently and knew that Regina had no intention of going back to Andrew. "What if we were to drop the subject of X-ray altogether, and switch to ultrasound instead? It's better than nothing."

"I can live with that," Andrew was truly concerned that his patient would leave JMH.

Leo, waiting for Regina's answer, spoke softly, "At least you wouldn't have to start all over with a new doctor."

"Let's walk over to ultrasound, Regina, and check the stone as well as taking a look at the baby. Don't you want to see the baby?" Andrew admired her strength, even if she was difficult to deal with.

Regina answered quietly, "Okay."

"Great, I'll page Frank and have him meet us there, I'm coming too," Frances was relieved.

Regarding the stone, the ultrasound revealed the same diagnosis. The baby appeared to be a perfectly normal boy! Regina wiped the tears from her face, and touched the screen. "We have your nursery ready, Frank Jr." Frank Sr. was the misty eyed one now. Regina continued, "It's a circus setting…..."

"Like my office, since your mummy became my patient," Andrew couldn't help sharing in the fun. "Now that the diagnosis of the stone is confirmed again, there will be no living with her!"

"We're going to have a grandson!" Frances stepped out to call Lamar, as Frank telephoned both sets of parents.

# Chapter Twenty
# Babies, Babies, Everywhere!

"Here comes the fall, dragging in the holidays," moaned a very tired Sylvia, over lunch at the Food Court in the mall.

"Let's have the holidays here, and bring the families to us this year," suggested Jeannie sympathetically, while checking her list for completion.

"That's fine with me," added Regina, "Monique hates to travel in the car."

When they returned home from shopping, Chuck was at the Solbergs' studying with Frank. "How would you guys feel about having the holidays in Miami this year, and letting the families come to us?" Jeannie was already relieved at the possibility of not traveling. Chuck shrugged, "I don't see why not, we've traveled every year since we've moved here."

"Sylvia's folks are already coming to help with the triplets; maybe they could come a little earlier!" Regina sounded hopeful.

Frank got up and danced around the living room, doing what resembled jumps of glee. "You're glad your parents are coming! That's good, Frank!" Jeannie interpreted.

"I'm glad we don't have a guest room! That's better, Jeannie," Frank corrected.

"I'll call Frances and see what she thinks," Regina laughed at seeing her husband so happy.

"Sure! The Mc Brides can stay with us for both celebrations. Lamar's son, Brain, is coming anyway." Frances was anxious to show off her lovely new house.

The Gerehauzers, who never left Miami for the holidays anyway, were delighted to be included.

Frank's side of the family would commute, as they had just fired their help again, and didn't trust new employees with their large inventory of pets. Adam and Marge were to celebrate the holidays at her family's mountain home this year, so they were delighted to be included with the "gang."

The plans fell smoothly into place; Thanksgiving would be at Isla Del Mar in the reception room, and Christmas would be at the Mac Michaels. Hazel and Frances were thrilled to be as highly regarded by the three younger couples as they were, and Sylvia's parents were always a delightful addition.

Menus were planned to exclude the three younger couples. "Not this year," Frances informed them; "there are plenty of us to prepare the food who are not pregnant." She, Hazel, Sis, Elizabeth, Andrea, Hyacinth, and Dorothy would handle the food. The three who were expecting, especially Sylvia, were ordered to relax.

Maternity clothes were traded back and forth, and holiday outfits were planned for comfort as well as appeal. Sylvia loved empire-waist styled maternity dresses, while Jeannie preferred the simple shift types. Regina preferred slacks and fancy flowing tops; but all three pregnant ladies always looked beautiful, and were complimented wherever they went.

Chuck and Jeannie had recently learned that they would also be having a boy. Planning to name their baby Charles, they knew he would most likely be called, Charlie. The genders of the Clements' triplets remained a surprise, but Sylvia had six names picked out to cover the bases either way.

Except for the Solberg seniors, the honored guests from out of town, arrived on the Wednesday before Thanksgiving. First things first, the men played golf while the ladies shopped at the International Mall. Next the visitors traveled between the Doral and Isla Del Mar to see the three nurseries. Everyone was amazed at the beauty and originality displayed in each of the three rooms. Although each of the nurseries was completely different, they all exuded, *"Welcome, we have all been anxiously waiting for you! We love you,"* to the tiny future occupants. The Big Top was invigorating! Cameras flashed in each home to preserve the memories. Dan was speechless when he saw his future grandson's nursery. "You two are sensational, and that's all there is to it," Andrea nodded in teary eyed agreement, while Elizabeth requested pictures. Bub and Sis, whispered, "Incredible;" upon learning that Regina made the Mache' decorations from flour, water, and newspaper. Elizabeth indicated the popcorn wagon, "Frank built that wagon out of wood and plexi glass, and that popcorn is also paper Mache'! "

Regina sat in the rocking chair every morning, while she prayed. She loved just being in the "big top," and couldn't wait to be holding her baby as she rocked in time to the nursery music that awaited him. Thanksgiving morning was especially moving for her. "Father, thanks for all that You give Your children. Let us honor You on this significant day, and always. Please keep Frank Jr., little Charlie, and the three wonders of Sylvia and Wyatt, safe, and let them continue to grow in Your love. Abba, please help all of us to remember that Dorothy and Raymond have feelings too, and keep us from any unkindness to them. Father, that sunrise is gorgeous! I love You."

Walking quietly to the kitchen for some orange juice, she encountered Frank coming in from the patio. "Look at the sunrise, Regina!"

"I have seen it already, but let's sit outside and enjoy it ," the glowing mother-to –be poured a second glass of juice.

"We have so much to be thankful for, Regina. Each other, the baby, our friends, our families, I could go on and on. I hope my mother doesn't cause any trouble today," Frank sipped his orange juice."

"He's on it," Regina looked at the breathtaking colors in the sky.

Chuck and Jeannie were outside too, and waved to their friends. Chuck motioned for them to come over, as it was too early to call from the patio.

Jeannie was taking muffins out of the oven when they entered. "Happy Thanksgiving, Frank kissed her cheek and handed her the pitcher of cold juice."

The friends embraced as though they hadn't seen each other in a long time. All were moved by the sunrise. "We take so much for granted," Chuck was thoughtful.

"What can we do to repay Him?" Jeannie asked nobody in particular.

"We might make a special effort to be more patient with their parents," Regina nodded toward the boys, who smiled. Jeannie's parents were staying with her, while Chuck's, by their own choice, were in a hotel. "That would be a special gift all right, all four are a challenge!" Chuck laughed.

"A challenge that we can have fun handling as a small team," Regina joined him.

Raising their glasses, Frank faced the sunset, "In Your honor we will not kill our parents on this special day." He then whispered, "I love You, awesome God."

Thanksgiving dinner was wonderful, <u>and everyone was kind to each other.</u> Moved by the silent efforts of the "special force team," the regulars went out of their way to welcome Dorothy and Ray Solberg, as well as Connie and Rob Nugent. Both couples were delighted with the nurseries. Over dinner the other guests, as if cued by God Himself, overlooked Dorothy's comments. "I warned Regina, that she better get someone in here to decorate that baby's room. We wanted a stimulating setting, and it's obvious that the resources knew just what they were doing." Dan looked at his daughter with admiration and bowed his head, "Thanks for looking after our little Pandemonium, God. Thank you for everything." Frances winked at him, as if she also knew Who was overseeing this feast.

Later in the evening, coffee and pies flooded the table, as Chuck's mother put her foot in her mouth. "Jeannie, we don't want the baby to be called Charlie!"

Before answering, Jeannie glanced at Regina for support. "Grandma's have the privilege of calling their grandchildren what they like," she gave her mother-in-law one her brightest smiles.

Sylvia looked unusually uncomfortable. I think the triplets are on the way, she smiled. Wyat, the mother-to-be, and Chuck left immediately for the hospital, while Leo called Andrew Kingsley at his home. Hanging up the phone, he followed the three others to JMH, with Hyacinth and Roger. Frank and Regina walked the Solbergs to their car, with packaged leftovers. After seeing them off, the younger Solbergs were also headed to the swiftly crowding waiting room at JMH.

Andrew Kingsley was already there and Sylvia was well on her way to becoming the first of the three mothers. Hyacinth Clements came into the world first, followed by her brother, Harper, six minutes later. Finally, Holly Clements, made her grand entrance, introducing herself with a loud cry. The delivery went smoothly and Sylvia was radiant. The adorable "litter" snuggled up contently to the exterior of their home for the last nine months. Harper squinted one eye open and sucked hard at his tiny fist, as his grandparents wept for joy. The group was gathered around Sylvia in silent awe, and in complete violation of hospital policy! Undisturbed, they continued a brief visit, until the nurses intervened to allow Sylvia to rest.

The crowd left chattering all the way home. It had been a remarkable day which ended with a phone call to Dorothy, including them in the excitement that they missed while driving home.

She seemed genuinely delighted to be included, and asked for Sylvia's address so she could send gifts to the new arrivals. Frank hugged his wife and told her how much he loved her. "Their babies are beautiful, Frank. I can't wait to hold them!"

"Don't worry, my love, we'll all get plenty of chances to do that! Three! They have three."

Bright and early the next morning, the Nativity set was displayed. The twinkling blue lights would once again help serve as a reminder of the Great Miracle, that took place in a humble manger, so many years ago. Regina felt the baby move inside her and touched her stomach gently. "He had no big top, sweet baby, but He is King of Heaven and Earth."

Regina went into the third bedroom to check on her laminated Christmas gifts that were drying. The two poems that she had written for Chuck and Jeannie and Sylvia and Wyatt, were ready to be wrapped. She noticed without concern that one of the plaques had been moved, but wondered why.

Christmas festivities were being planned, including a party for *The Musical Cons.* Warden Robertson and Mindy hand delivered invitations to Frances and Regina at the clinic. Frances noticed that the couple looked extraordinarily happy, and couldn't help concluding that Santa's upcoming visit wasn't entirely responsible.

Gordon winked at her and motioned to a small box in his pocket. Hugging her, he whispered, it's an engagement ring, for Christmas!"

Holiday goodies were on every counter at work and plentiful at every home as well. Because they were so active, Regina and Jeannie had gained very little weight during their pregnancies. Christmas carols playing among the decorations, kept everyone in a holiday mood. Jeannie was visiting Regina and Frances at work and commented, "My dad has been hiding in the back room of Wyatt's office lately, working on surprises. Sylvia doesn't have a clue what he's doing, and her parents told me to mind my own bis-NESS," she tried to copy Hyacinth's adorable Jamaican accent!

The tiny triplets were dressed in emerald green, for Christmas Eve and would wear red the next day. Resembling little dolls, they were content being passed among the large group of friends. Sylvia looked lovely and had already dropped a good bit of her weight. Her parents were contemplating a move to Miami. "They realize that they'll miss too much living so far away," Sylvia was delighted with the possibility of their relocation.

Christmas morning started early with the usual trip to the nursery to pray.

Against the back hall wall, adjacent to the door of the big top, Regina saw the exquisite ringmaster doll that stood four feet tall. Smiling broadly, he pointed to the oak information sign propped under his left hand. On the top of the sign, an intricately carved cherub held a tray of bright red candy apples. The small angel had indulged in the wares, as evidenced by the half eaten candy on the stick in his hands, and the tell tale red sugar melted on his little face. Beneath him was the same poem Regina was giving her dearest friends.

# The Little Miracle

God looked at His creations, and He smiled at each one,
The sun and moon were beautiful, the planets were all done.
His tiny stars would sparkle, in the darkest evening sky,
The softest rains would speak to Earth, and flowers would reply.

He knew His lovely lands in green, would soon dress up in snow.
The mountains and the oceans, had their own majestic glow.
The valleys and the forests, with their tall and graceful trees;
His stormy winter blizzards, and the gentle summer breeze.

He cherished every animal, each in a special way,
And dearly loved the man and wife, He'd made the other day.
Now watching them together, in the garden, hand in hand,
He planned a little miracle, more glorious than grand.

The man and wife would change their names to "parents," to allow,
The love and great protection, for the gift He'd send them now.
So on His master drawing board, He sketched it from the start,
This special little miracle would touch each human heart.

Now as with each of all His works; no two were just the same.
And so for "little miracle," He chose a special name.
And "baby," was the word He used, and with His holy touch,
He outlined that small figure, of the gift He'd love so much!

And then He told the softest cloud, that it was to begin,
To fashion special formulas, to make His baby's skin.
He reached up toward the sunset, and took a little trace,
Of color, from the gorgeous tones, and placed them in your face.

Now seeking out the rarest gems, He called them to the skies,
For polishing and blessing, to become His baby's eyes.
He then sent for His flowers, and from all of them, He chose,
The smallest of His blossoms, to become your little nose.

He called together every ray of sun – It was worthwhile!
Because this glorious display; became your little smile.
And next, selecting cherub's harps, He tuned them up with care,
And set the pattern and the pace, to spin His baby's hair.

He found two little music notes, that had been lost for years,
And kissed them both, and made them into tiny baby ears.
Commanding every ocean to perform, He chose a part,
Of easy tide, and made the rhythm, for your little heart.

Then noticing a little deer, with gentle eyes, He took,
That picture of pure innocence, to fashion your same look.
He listened in the forest, and heard nature's lullaby,
And made a new, effective song – "The Little Baby's Cry."

And now upon completion, He was glad He'd saved a space,
Of rarest golden sunshine, which will be your mother's face.

By Regina Louise Solberg

The card was signed, *The Stripe Clad Bumblebees.* Frank had described the nursery to *The Musical Cons,* during a practice. The three inmates that Regina had called aside, organized the group. Together they had acquired the supplies and designed, crafted, and painted the wooden sign. Imported from France, the doll was from Frances and Lamar. Regina was speechless. She turned around to see Frank armed with the camera. After snapping her picture, he hugged and kissed his wife." Frances and Lamar made me promise to catch you on film."

The day was filled with love, and the Birthday Boy was ever present among the large gathering of friends and family. The Newspaper had asked permission to cover the gift from *The Musical Cons*, and they were granted entrance on that special Christmas morning. Following the story and flashes from the cameras, the reporter added, "Warden Gordon Robertson and his new fiancée Melinda Thompson, are present, and have accepted an invitation to the Mac Michaels' home for Christmas dinner. "New Years is at our house," Mindy gushed. Everyone was in agreement and shared the happy story of the engagement at the prison!

During dinner, Wyatt stood and made an announcement. "Friends and family – Scratch that! Family and extended family, Bert has been working on three gifts that he feels are not good enough to present! I am hoping with a round of reassuring applause that we can get 'The Little Drummer Boy,' to play for us." Jeannie's father bowed his head and humbly retrieved the brown paper bag that he intended to just leave behind after the holidays. The contents were three hand painted door signs for the nurseries:

Jeannie's was a farm of adorable baby animals. A toddler dressed in overalls, with his bottle in the back pocket, was posting a sign, "Welcome to Charlie's Farm."

Sylvia's was a picture of a wooden shoe set on blue waves. A flag reading, *Winken, Blinkin, and Nod,* flew from the top of the "boat," introducing the three little passengers who were wearing sailor hats that read, Hyacinth, Harper and Holly.

The third was in the shape of a ticket, picturing circus features; that said, *Frankie's Big Top.* It would be hung on the door that night.

Everyone was tearfully applauding. Connie, walking over to hug the artist, looked over her shoulder at her daughter-in-law. "Well don't just stand there, Jeannie, she sobbed, "Call the baby store and order T-shirts that say Charlie!"

Regina carefully packed the nativity for next year, and stored the left over holiday goodies in the freezer. Answering the phone, she regretted popping the cookie in her mouth. It was Chuck, calling to say that they were on the way to Trinity.

Jeannie did not have an easy delivery, but labored in vain, as the obstetrician shook his head. "The baby is headed for fetal distress, Jeannie; we must get him out of there."

"Do whatever is best for him," the exhausted patient panted.

Eight minutes later, Charlie was delivered by Caesarian section without complications. Chuck came out of the operating room glowing, as the nurse followed pushing the bassinette with his sleeping replica toward the nursery.

The group went down to the cafeteria for supper, while Jeannie rested in recovery.

Frank wondered if Regina would be alright. She had many incidents of renal colic throughout the pregnancy, and labor and delivery was not always a piece of cake. His anticipation was short termed though, as Regina went into labor eighteen hours after Jeannie.

There were no private labor rooms at JMH, and many people were waiting in the hall. Regina was placed in a ward of six screaming women. She couldn't understand why they were screaming, but made no comment. Andrew was in surgery completing an emergency C-section, and Frank was beside himself. Regina started with the patient next to her. "Are you okay, honey?" she asked.

The young Haitian girl looked up at her, and screamed again.

"You know, if you take a deep breath through your nose like this," Pollyanna demonstrated, "and let it out through your mouth, blowing this napkin as you go, the pain will take care of itself."

The young girl just screamed again.

Regina helped her move up against the pillow and placed the napkin in her hand. "Now you try it," she smiled.

The frightened girl, held Regina's hand tightly as she drew the deep breath.

Letting it out, she blew the napkin and smiled weakly.

The laboring missionary moved on to the next bed and repeated the instruction, as the ward nurse came rushing into the room, " Mrs. Solberg, your doctor will have our heads! You weren't supposed to be in here!"

"I'm always where I'm supposed to be," Regina smiled.

Frank, and the nurse whom he had summoned, helped Regina back onto her own bed and moved her to the private room that Leo had just demanded.

The labor was slow, but within normal limits. Regina was getting bored.

Andrew warned Frank, "Keep her busy in here, before she starts a band in the indigent ward!" Leaving the room, he laughed. He had come to love his troublesome patient, but she wasn't out of the woods yet. Six hours later, Andrew escorted the stretcher to the delivery room. Frank Jr. was handed to Regina directly after his brief, uncomplicated birth. She looked at her baby and commented, "You're the picture of your sweet father."

The crisp British accent answered, "Let's hope you take after him if you ever need to see a doctor!"

"I'm going home as soon as they get him cleaned up," Regina was already sitting up."

"I'm going to retire, before she gets pregnant again," the weary Andrew laughed.

# Chapter Twenty-One
# Turn the Other Cheek

The three girls were always together at one house or the other. They were having a ball playing with their babies and taking them out to show the world how beautiful they were. Any excuse to spend the day at the International Mall with strollers and fully stocked diaper bags, was welcomed by the three new mothers.

Sylvia's triplets were cappuccino colored, with soft dark curls, and Charlie had a deep olive complexion, and big dark brown eyes. Frank Jr. on the other hand, was a fair skinned, towhead, with bright blue eyes! The families laughed, but were glad that both sets of great-grandparents had blue eyes, since Frank and Regina both had dark brown, and so did both sets of their parents! The group of babies was exquisite, and by passers couldn't help raving about them. Surrounded by love around the clock by their huge fan club at home, they were socially alert and unusually happy.

Dreading their return to work, the three mothers avoided the topic. Each had bonded deeply to their new arrivals, and couldn't bear the thought of missing a moment of time with them.

Except for the blue eyes, Frank Jr. was a clone of his father! "Exactly where is Regina's DNA?" Dan teased Frank, "and who contributed the skin tone?"

"I was very fair skinned as a child," Frank Sr. boasted.

Charlie was his father made over, and the triplets were a combination of their attractive parents.

Leo Gerehauzer, to his own surprise, had grown to love Regina like his own, and the other women similarly. He was becoming increasingly concerned about their burden of separating from the babies, which was obvious to others, no matter how the girls tried to minimize it. One Saturday, after golf, he and Hazel met with the three new mothers and Frances. "I'm concerned about JMH if you two stay out too long," the colonel looked at Jeannie and Regina. Continuing, he addressed Sylvia, "And you must be missed at your job too. Am I right?"

"Yes Sir," Sylvia answered.

"Now I know you haven't been on leave that long, but what I'm proposing takes time," Leo explained. "Regina, what do you and Frances think of starting a hospital day care center; a very exclusive, state of the art, daycare center."

Regina and Frances were flabbergasted! "I would love it!" Both answered at once.

"Hazel asked me earlier if she might be needed as well," Leo added taking his wife's hand.

"Absolutely!" Frances was delighted for the second time in the last few minutes.

There was wing of the hospital close to the Department of Orthopedics that never opened, and Leo had already approached the Board of Directors with his new idea. "We could make the facility available to our house staff, and use a portion of the income to hire base employees to work there. The bulk of the staff can be clinical students from the university who need hours in Early Childhood Development. Extra profits would be for JMH to use. The three women, who I think could set up the whole show, would send their children free of charge. The center would also be an incentive to keep top notch medical personnel at JMH, once their educations are completed."

When the Board of Directors realized that the "three ladies" he mentioned, were the very ones who formed *The Musical Cons*, they voted unanimously; and Leo was immediately granted full reign. "You three can certainly decorate the place and Hazel and Frances could start interviews next week," Leo had put a great deal of thought into this, and Regina loved him for it. "Well?"

Leo shouted, causing everyone to jump out of their skin, as he laughed at them.

"I'm in," Regina was ready to start immediately.

"I'm in," Jeannie was on her feet.

"Me too," Sylvia stood shyly.

"Count on me," Frances picked up Frank Jr.

"And me," Hazel grabbed one of the two crying triplets.

The ladies swarmed him with tearful hugs of relief, and then each other.

Regina quietly bowed her head, "My Abba, you spoil me! I love You, and I thank you for the marvelous people we are surrounded by."

"Regina Louise," came the familiar army bellow again.

"Sir, Yes Sir," the feisty redhead saluted.

"Do you intend to share a conversation with God with all of us?"

"Sir, Yes Sir," she responded, as everyone bowed their heads.

"Our Father, I turn this prayer over to Your wonderful son, Leo."

Leo took over, "God, thank you for our family! We ask for Your guidance in this new endeavor, and we pray for babies everywhere."

Three boys were delighted with the idea of the daycare, and Wyatt couldn't believe they would have no cost. "None," Sylvia relayed the information.

The five ladies would meet at Frances's house tomorrow for lunch, and set to work. Lamar would help with any building needs, and Frank was very handy in that field as well.

The babies were happy in swings on the patio, while their mothers and second grandmothers talked over lunch. Hazel started the discussion, "Girls, how do you feel about using your three nursery themes, with different decorations, of course?"

Frances followed, "Be honest, now. If it would bother any of you for any reason, there are many other themes that could be used."

"I have absolutely no problem with the idea, and it would cut our work in half,"

Regina realized that time was of the essence.

"Of course," Jeannie added, "there are countless ways to set our themes that wouldn't necessarily duplicate them."

"Oh yes," Sylvia confirmed.

Hazel looked up over her glasses, "Regina, may we use your poem?"

"Sure," the flattered author blushed.

The ladies chattered on until everything was pretty well organized. The infant nursery was to be nursery rhymes, the toddler room was to be baby farm animals, and the little hooligans in preschool, would be fittingly housed in the big top!

"How goes it?" Leo telephoned in to check on the progress.

"We're just asking Regina to give us an idea for the lunch/craft room."

Regina was very modest, and wanted everyone else to give their ideas. It was the same with the nurseries. While they were all Regina's creations, she made each mother feel like they did theirs themselves.

"Well, Pollyanna?" Frances looked at her "daughter" with growing pride.

"What do you guys think?" Regina respectfully included everyone.

Hazel loved Regina, "I think that if you don't cough up an idea from that crowded inventory in your gorgeous head, I'm calling the colonel!"

Pursing her lips, the unthreatened new mother answered, "How about Small World?"

"What about Small World?" Sylvia was all ears.

"Well we could have a huge Paper Mache' globe hanging on the wall, with small dolls set on it from different countries. Below the globe we might have an ocean with giant crayons sailing in it carrying more international dolls. We add a few bright hot air balloons with more multi-cultural children waving from the bas-kets, and the rest would be small details."

"That would be gorgeous," Jeannie was always the first one to cry.

Protective second mother, Frances, spoke authoritatively, "That is an adorable idea, honey, but JMH can buy the dolls from the shop at the International Mall, they are not using yours."

Regina loved this lady! "That would most likely be alright with them, we're talking about toys that we can animate with very little effort, and the hospital, after all would keep all of the decorations."

Dennis De Sanko was still trying to redeem himself, "Dr. Gerehuazer, we should have Orthopedics sponsor this operation, and use the publicity for ourselves."

"That's up to my stolen daughter, Regina," the colonel still resented the  spineless administrator.

Dennis asked to speak with Frances first, and then Regina. "That's fine with us," Frances snapped, "but Regina is an artist, so we will be buying two of each doll;

one for her to work with at home and keep as her personal inventory, and one for your décor."

"Consider that a must," the administrator knew who to kiss up to.

Regina was thrilled, as were her friends. She had a passion for dolls, especially multicultural types, and hoped to have a daugh-ter someday, to share her collection with.

"Alright, Sonny, looks like you've got yourself a deal, but we'll need a credit card."

"I'll bring one over myself," the coward answered and continued, "I haven't seen the babies in a couple of weeks."

The work began and the five women were having the time of their lives. Hazel rubbed her husband's shoulders, "Frances and I were thinking that we could hire Jeannie or Regina to supervise the center."

"Jeannie," he answered authoritatively, "Regina is needed in Orthopedics."

"That's what we thought!" Hazel was enjoying her work, and it showed.

"Sylvia also wants to work as the head of the Infant Nursery. She is devastated by the thought of leaving her babies, and she is tired of court work."

"That's fine too. Listen, do you think Regina will be hurt if the other two work there and she's with us?"

"No, because we've already discussed it; Regina is going to be the Chairman of the Board, and given the proximity of the center, she can come and go as she pleases."

"You're sure?"

"Yes, she also likes to be with Frank Sr., and the position that she will be in  allows her to dote on both Franks!"

The following week, The Child Enrichment Center was opening and the two boys were graduating from medical school. Regina bought Frank a new set of golf clubs for the occasion, and Jeannie

got Chuck a new sound system. The exceptionally moving ceremony was followed by a glamorous celebration at Frances and
Lamar's. Dorothy was in her typical, "my son the doctor," role
and made the mistake of bashing Regina. "This daycare is just
manipulation to be with Frank Jr. instead of working. If Frank
can't be with the baby all day, she shouldn't either!"

It was Leo who answered, although Dan was ready to do
it himself.

"Dorothy, do you ever shut that gaping mouth of yours?
Regina was not the mastermind behind the <u>Child Enrichment
Center</u>, as it is now known. We were.

Instead of admiring your daughter-in-law's talents you re-
peatedly attempt to crush them. You are in the wrong company
for that nonsense, sister."

Typically when the colonel shouted orders, there was total
silence, and this time was no exception. The Solbergs were furious, but eventually laughed lightly. Dorothy knew that Frank
would now be on a payroll. If "the kids" bucked her before, what
would stop them now? Frances was close to flight and Dan left
the room. He met Regina out on the patio covering her mouth to
keep the laughter back, and he was in the same condition.

Frank collapsed on the couch exhausted. The fourth year of
medical school had been difficult; and now he would begin an
internship at JMH in the fall, as would Chuck. While both new
doctors were delighted, they knew how demanding those schedules would be. "At least we'll get paid now, and we'll be close to
the babies, so we can see them during the day," Frank tried to look
on the bright side of things.

"Yeah but this is the worst year, then it starts to go downhill!" Chuck tried to sound encouraging.

The summer had been filled with excitement over the new center, but the couples still found plenty of time to socialize. Frank was on the hand service and Chuck returned to histories and physicals. Both were very happy with their lovely families and that would make it easier to soldier on to the finish line. Wyatt was a tower of encouragement and Leo was more like a father to Frank than Raymond was.

Once internship started, the hectic schedules began. Regina was happy that she had opted to remain on in the Department of Orthopedics, as that did enable her to see Frank far more than she would if she had moved. The couple loved each other immensely, and it showed in everything they did. Frank was not used to the exhaustion that internship carried with it. Born with a silver spoon in his mouth, he never had to rough it. This was no dance party; it was excruciating hours of cold hard work, and it tried the souls of the toughest.

Rotating through Orthopedics was a welcome change for Frank. He was not fond of being spoken to like a "scut-puppy," and that was the case for interns on every other service in the hospital. He seemed brighter on this service, and Regina loved the change in him. Dinner on the patio was always a treat and Monique loved the attention she always got there. "There is a ninety year old Cuban lady with a hip fracture that I'm assigned to," Frank was explaining. "She has the nicest family, and they treat me with such respect."

"Cuban families are usually very close, and they are very respectful to medical personnel. I love it when they are in our clinic."

Frank's pager went off, as Regina served desert.

"Okay, honey, I'll tell you what, I'll come in to check on her myself."

The patient's granddaughter was worried about her. Regina couldn't help admiring the care that her husband took of his patients.

"Are you okay with me going in to check on her? I'm not required to, but I think it's a good idea, especially since I want a residency here."

"By all means, go," Regina kissed him.


Frank did not finish at the hospital until 3:00am and had to be back in three hours for rounds. Regina packed his lunch and told herself that he would be okay. Sylvia called Regina in the clinic to report that Frank Jr. had a high fever. "I'll call his pediatrician," the concerned mother answered, as her husband walked in for lunch.

"Honey, I have to take Frank Jr. to the doctor."

"I'll come with you; I'm done for the day."

Answering his page, he went to the phone on the desk. "Well, I have a sick baby, so I'm going to have to leave to take him to the doctor, but I'll call the nurses myself to have them check the tubing."

Frances looked up from her charts, "What's wrong?"

"A patient on our service with a broken hip has a very caring family. The granddaughter is concerned that her I V line may be clogged."

Frances was suspicious, "Let me go over there myself, Frank. You take the baby to the doctor."

"Thanks so much. Her name is Maria Rodriguez, she is 1102."

Maria Rodriguez was a very sweet, frail lady who appeared to be resting quietly. There was no problem with the line at all. Her granddaughter, Eva Rodriguez, was the one who had called Frank. She stroked her grandmother's hair as she explained to Frances how great "Frank" had been to them. "I'm hoping that he will stop back in after he takes his son to the doctor," she smiled.

"Well, your grandmother is doing fine, dear," Frances forced herself to smile back. "I don't know about you," the wise nurse added, "but if I were sleeping, I would find somebody stroking the hair off my head annoying."

On the way to the doctor, Frank Jr. pulled a yellow envelope from his father's lab coat pocket, which hung on the hook above the back door near his car seat. "Oh no, honey," Regina laughed taking the envelope from her son. "What is that?" Frank yawned.

"I don't know," Regina saw nothing on the outside.

"Open it, will you?"

"Sure," she carefully opened the expensive paper.

Inside the envelope was a card with a sunset on it, on the inside was the message: *Anytime, Anywhere!* No signature.

Frank was clearly shocked, and Regina believed him to be.

"Where was your lab coat?" She asked calmly.

"On me, except for a few minutes during rounds, when I hung it in the nurse's station to help relocate a shoulder."

"Well be careful where you leave it."

Frank was close to tears, as he adored his wife and their baby, and this was not a welcomed greeting card, by any stretch of the imagination.

The pediatrician found an ear infection and gave the baby antibiotics. He commented on how advanced Frank Jr.'s development was for a baby so young.

Frank explained the child enrichment center at JMH. The older doctor nodded approvingly.

On the way home the pager went off again. Frank returned the call to hear Eva Rodriguez's frantic concerns about her grandmother's sutures.

"Let me call the desk and get someone in there," the exasperated intern answered.

"She's ninety years old, Frank, and she wants you," the granddaughter persisted.

"Eva I can't come in right now, but I will send the nurses."

Regina gave Frank Jr. his medicine and put him to bed. The gorgeous little boy smiled at her as he finished his bottle and drifted to sleep under the big top. Frank had gone downstairs to the café for Cuban sandwiches for dinner. Regina called Frances, and while relaying the events of the afternoon, she burst into tears.

"I'll call you right back, honey." Frances _burst_ into room 1102. "What seems to be the problem now, young lady?" The irritated army nurse glared.

"It's her sutures," Eva smiled, "I think they are bothering her."

"That's odd, because she has no sutures," Frances was merciless, "She has staples, and they're fine."

"Oh, I'm so sorry. I'm just very fond of my grandmother, and I want the best for her. Will the doctor be in tonight?"

"You better believe it, sweetmeat!" Frances called Leo's office from the room.

Meeting Leo in the hall she relayed the first name basis relationship that the visitor was using to address Frank. "She calls constantly and there was a mysterious card found in Frank's lab coat pocket." Finishing the details, she walked to the desk. Did anyone see a visitor place a card in Dr. Solberg's lab coat pocket this morning?" Nobody had, which was not surprising, given the fact that morning rounds were always a madhouse. She stepped into an empty room and called Regina. Frank was back from the café, so the call was naturally about the baby. "I'll see you in the morning, honey," the licensed meddler was on the prowl!

Leo assured Eva Rodriguez that her grandmother was fine, and had Frank pulled from the case, relocating the young intern to Pediatric Orthopedics. He dropped by Isla Del Mar on his way home and told Frank that he thought some experience with George Easterlin would be beneficial. "George is in charge of the resident program, and it wouldn't hurt to bump elbows with him." He exchanged pagers with Frank, winked at Regina, and went home for dinner.

Eva was furious to hear that a new doctor would be taking over - a female intern! She tried to page Frank, who had been given a new pager. She went to the desk to ask for his pager number, but was told that she could not obtain that information. Visiting the Child Enrichment Center, she brought a gift for Frank Jr. "His father was so kind to my grandmother," she explained prettily, "and I would love to say thanks in person. Does he come here to pick the baby up?"

"No, his mother picks him up, and I cannot allow you to see the baby without their permission," Sylvia didn't like the sound or looks of the situation.

"Which one is he?" the visitor stood on tip toes.

"I'm sorry ma'am, but you cannot be here."

Eva left the package and went back to her grandmother's room, hoping to run into Frank on the way.

The present she left had a card on it that matched the card found in Frank's lab coat pocket. This one read, "*To Daddy's Pride and Joy.*" Frank destroyed the card and handed the gift to Regina. It was a little piggy bank that wore a bib saying, "Somebody loves you." The poor little bank was smashed to powder by somebody's father. Regina laughed, but tried to calm her husband down.

"This is bound to happen, honey. Patients become infatuated with their doctors all the time."

Weeks passed without further incident, before Frank Solberg was paged to the emergency room. Answering the page, the clerk told him that someone was there to see him. When Frank asked who was there, the clerk responded quietly, "Doctor, this lady said that if you should ask me who she is, to say that you should just come and see for yourself!"

"The emergency room is not a malt shop," Frank answered angrily, "I am busy with my patients."

Eva handed the clerk a letter cackling, "Just give this to Frank, or better yet, give it to Mrs. Solberg!" She turned on her heels and pranced out the door.

Regina went to the emergency room and retrieved the letter. "Thank you," she said sweetly. If anyone would have had any suspicion, they didn't now. Taking the letter back to the clinic, she read it privately. *"Frank, I must see you. I am pregnant and we must discuss what we are going to do about it. I will not have an abortion."*

The JMH chapel was a quiet and soothing place, and Regina loved to be there. Bowing her head, she cried softly, "Abba please help us through this, if it is in fact true. I love You, and I love my husband and our baby. The letter was given to me," she sobbed, "do I tell him or should I simply destroy it? It could certainly be a trap to cause trouble between us. Please give me some answers, Sweet Abba, and stay right by me, as I am frightened. I wish more than anything that our marriage will stay strong."

Wiping her face, Regina returned to clinic, and as she passed the gift shop she noticed a plaque. It was a picture of a beautiful rainbow over a placid babbling brook. The saying across it was: "You are never given a wish, without also being given the power to make it come true," by Richard Bach. "Thank you my Abba," she smiled shredding the letter as she dropped it into the trash can. "I must start by forgiving this lady, and I ask You to help me with that, as right now I am very angry with her and would relish the opportunity to rip her hair out by the roots."

Once at the clinic, Regina told Frances everything that had just occurred. "I would ignore it and see what happens, honey," the wise second mother advised, "that's the oldest trick in the book."

"I don't believe for a minute that she and Frank had an affair, but I really wish she would stop dropping by here."

"She'll get tired of making the trip for nothing, and Frank is smart enough to screen his pages," Frances reassured. She then left for the gift shop knowing that most of their novelty items like the plaque Regina just saw were unique and one time only.

Regina left the clinic to visit The Child Enrichment Center across the hall. Frank was just getting ready to do a puppet show for his son's class and had already been to the pre-school and toddler rooms. He picked his son up and kissed him. Realizing that Regina had entered the room, he hugged and kissed her too. Taking the wise army nurse's advice, she sat comfortably on the floor with Frank Jr. to enjoy the show.

Volume Two

# The First Mrs. Solberg

## Chapter One
## The Extra Fidestrial

The last four and one half years had been wonderful in Miami, and Regina loved it there. While medical school was a grind, it was also filled with marvelous memories. Internship was more demanding, but at least Frank would be paid now. Occasionally she wondered if a move would be a good decision, and had discussed the possibility with him. The letter delivered by Eva Rodriguez months ago, lurked around every corner in her mind.

> "Frank, I must see you. I am pregnant and we must discuss what we are going to do about it; I will not have an abortion."

While she didn't believe the messenger was telling the truth, she was still bothered by the fact that this brazen woman lived in the same city as they did.

Eva Rodriguez was the granddaughter of one of Frank's former patients. She was infatuated with him to the point of making pop up visits around the hospital in an attempt to bump into him. Although he had made it crystal clear that he was not interested in her, she persisted tirelessly, until she finally realized that the strategically placed blockades, were impassable.

There was North Carolina and its gorgeous mountains, which enticed her. Their close friends were here in Miami though, and it seemed foolish to run from something that would probably never even materialize. Her best friend, Jeannie, had a similar temptation to leave the area, triggered from a hospital employee who had relentlessly chased Chuck during the first year of medical school. Elena Garcia, a ward clerk at the hospital and the daughter of a prominent nephrology attending, couldn't resist married men. She went so far as to follow Chuck home using the excuse that her uncle lived in the same building. Finally she subsided, but Jeannie was never completely assured that she would not return to her old games. Having transferred from a nursing position, Jeannie was now working at the Child Enrichment Center affiliated with Jackson Memorial Hospital. She was delighted to be able to work with her new baby Charlie, but concerned that she could no longer keep her eye on things at JMH. Although she continually tried to reassure herself that her troubles with the prowler were over, the haunting attempts still came to mind on a regular basis.

The two girls shared their worries and had both concluded that their husbands were strong, faithful men and that moving would not guarantee that other women wouldn't chase them in another location. They had far too much to lose with all the beautiful friends they had in Miami and the golden opportunity for residency programs here, in a facility that was as well-known as Jackson Memorial Hospital.

Regina and her "second mother," Frances, were enjoying a cup of coffee after a very busy clinic.

Frank came bursting into her office excited by the news, "I have been offered one of the two spots for an Orthopedic residency here but," he added taking a deep breath, "I need to give George Easterlin my answer in 'six minutes!' The program is too competitive to wait for acceptance."

"Well what did you tell George?" Regina asked, annoyed.

"I told him that it wasn't only my decision, and that you were considering the mountains."

"I think it's ridiculously unreasonable for him to allow you six minutes to make a decision that lasts four years! They loved you in Chapel Hill and are willing to wait for your decision."

"So I'll tell him, no. Look, sweetheart, you have stood by me for almost five years, no questions asked. It's your turn to decide where we live."

"Don't tell him, no, Frank. What do you really want to do?"

"Stay here. The program is one of the best in the country and Chuck just signed up for his residency in internal medicine. Above all though, I want you and Frank Jr. to be happy."

"Then tell him, yes. Our friends are here, and so are both families."

"On second thought, I'll tell him, no." Frank laughed. "Are you sure, honey?"

"Yes, I am sure. We'll stay here at least for the next four years."

"Lamar will be pleased that we won't have to move now either," Frances laughed, but wasn't joking.

Hugging her, Frank practically ran out of the office to tell George Easterlin that he would gladly accept the position. Regina turned to Frances, "When I see George Easterlin, I'm going to give him a piece of my mind, attending physician or not! I don't care how great he is, he should be more considerate!"

"I can see why you're upset, honey," Frances answered. "The faculty around here can be downright snobs. They know we have the best program and make no bones about using that leverage. They have had their sights set for Frank since he was a first year student."

Moments later the door opened and George Easterlin walked in, his blue eyes dancing with delight. The attending knew that adding Frank Solberg to his staff was a valuable asset and that the Orthopedic Residency Program would benefit greatly by it. Moving toward Regina, he extended his hand for a warm welcome and congratulations. Regina stood, and shaking hands she said, "Thank you so much for considering Frank, Sir, he is delighted."

Frances looked up, smiling. Relieved that the Solbergs were staying in Miami, she laughed, "That's telling him!" The two women hugged each other as the confused attending stood by.

"Did I miss something?" he asked with a twinkle in his eye. "Men are born missing something," Frances answered gruffly but grinning. "I'm just glad I don't have to relocate since my adopted daughter and her husband will be here for at least another four years! Come on, Regina, let's go steal a few minutes with Frank Jr. while we tell Jeannie the good news."

Frank Solberg and Chuck Nugent had completed medical school, started Internship, and were now preparing for the second half of the haul toward the completion of their careers. Frank would specialize in Orthopedic Surgery and Chuck in Internal medicine. Wyatt Clements, another close friend, was thriving in his new practice as an Ophthalmologist, having finished his training only a few years ago at Bascom Palmer Eye Institute, where he met Regina and Frances. He and his wife Sylvia had a set of triplets. Sylvia had transferred from her work as a court reporter to the head of the infant nursery at the Child Enrichment Center. The center was recently opened at Jackson Memorial Hospital at the request of Leo Gerehauzer, for the three young couples' new babies as well as for the children of the house staff. The three younger couples were as bonded as any family might be and were extremely close to the two older couples that shared their group of ten. Leo Gerehauzer was the attending physician who headed the Orthopedic Hand Service. A former army Colonel, he and his wife Hazel adored the young Solbergs. Frances McNeal Mac Michaels was Regina's "second mother," and her husband Lamar, was Regina's step-father's retired former business partner and close friend.

The entire close- knit group was having dinner at the Rustic Inn Crab House tonight, accompanied by all five babies! Regina was closing the clinic area while Grandma Frances went to get Frank Jr., when the telephone on the desk rang. "Outpatient clinic, Mrs. Solberg speaking."

"Oh, hi, Regina, this is Carolee from Dr. Easterlin's office. There is a gentleman here to see Frank," she whispered into the receiver, "I think that he is a process server."

A native of Flushing, New York, Michele Menard has traveled all over the world, embracing different cultures along the way. She has four children, and following an exhausting seventeen year divorce battle, has managed to still love her former husband. Enjoying a very close relationship with God, she can usually find humor in almost any situation!

CPSIA information can be obtained at www.ICGtesting.com
Printed in the USA
BVOW09s1504151114

375240BV00003B/11/P